Battles

THAT CHANGED THE MODERN WORLD

DALE ANDERSON

RSVP

RAINTREE
STECK-VAUGHN
P U B L I S H E R S
The Steck-Vaughn Company

Austin, Texas

Consultant: Gary Gerstle, Department of History, The Catholic University of America

Developed for Steck-Vaughn Company by
Visual Education Corporation, Princeton, New Jersey

Project Director: Jewel Moulthrop
Assistant Editor: Emilie McCardell
Researcher: Carol Ciaston
Photo Research: Photosearch, Inc.
Production Supervisor: Maryellen Filipek
Proofreading Management: Amy Davis
Word Processing: Cynthia C. Feldner
Interior Design: Lee Grabarczyk
Cover Design: Maxson Crandall
Page Layout: Maxson Crandall, Lisa R. Evans

Raintree Steck-Vaughn Publishers staff

Editor: Shirley Shalit
Project Manager: Joyce Spicer

Library of Congress Cataloging-in-Publication Data

Anderson, Dale, 1953–
    Battles that changed the modern world / Dale Anderson
        p.   cm. — (20 Events)
    Includes bibliographical references and index.
    Summary: Presents highlights of twenty battles that changed the modern world, including the three days at Gettysburg, the bombing of Guernica, the Tet offensive, and the Six-Day War.
    ISBN 0-8114-4928-9
    1. Battles—Juvenile literature.   2. Military history, Modern—19th century—Juvenile literature.   3. Military history, Modern—20th century—Juvenile literature.   [1. Battles. 2. Military history, Modern—19th century.   3. Military history, Modern—20th century.]   I. Title.   II. Title: Battles that changed the modern world.   III. Series.
D361.A53 1994   93–17028
904′.7—dc20   CIP
                                                                AC

Printed and bound in the United States

  2 3 4 5 6 7 8 9 0   VH   99 98 97 96 95 94

Cover: The terrible Civil War that killed hundreds of thousands of people and destroyed large portions of the nation ended on April 9, 1865. (Inset) In the small Virginia village of Appomattox, Confederate general Robert E. Lee surrendered his remaining troops to Union general Ulysses S. Grant.

Credits and Acknowledgments

Cover photos: Anne S. K. Brown Military Collection, Brown University Library (background), *Peace In Union,* oil painting by Thomas Nast, Galena/Jo Daviess County Historical Society (inset)
Illustrations: American Composition and Graphics
Maps: Parrot Graphics

5: Musée Legion d'Honneur/Bulloz (left), Walker Art Gallery, Liverpool (right); **7:** Anne S. K. Brown Military Collection, Brown University Library (left), Lincoln Museum/Lincoln National Corporation (right); **9:** Henry Groskinsky (left), Larry Sherer/High Impact/*The Civil War: Gettysburg* © 1985 Time-Life Books, Inc. (right); **10:** Anne S. K. Brown Military Collection, Brown University Library; **11:** Private Collection (left), Archiv für Kunst und Geschichte, Berlin (right); **12:** Monroe County Historical Society (left), Southwest Museum (right); **13:** The Bettmann Archive; **14:** Victoria and Albert Museum/Art Resource; **15:** Novosti/Sovfoto (left), The Bettmann Archive (right); **16:** Archiv für Kunst und Geschichte, Berlin (left), Tallendier (right); **17:** Smithsonian Institution; **18:** Agencia Efe, Madrid; **19:** Centro de Arté Reina Sofia National Museum, Madrid/Art Resource, © SPADEM/ARS, N.Y.; **20:** UPI/Bettmann (left), Sovfoto/Eastfoto (right); **21:** The Bettmann Archive; **22:** Imperial War Museum, London; **23:** U.S. Air Force (left), UPI/Bettmann (right); **24:** National Archives (left), Ullstein (right); **26:** Tokyo University Museum of Fine Arts, Tokyo/© Konichi Yasuda; **27:** U.S. Navy Combat Art Collection; **29:** Novosti/The Bettmann Archive (left), Sovfoto (right); **30:** UPI/Bettmann; **31:** U.S. Navy Combat Art Collection; **32:** Sovfoto/Eastfoto; **33:** Ooksin/Sipa Press (left), Alain Evrard/Photo Researchers (right); **34:** UPI/Bettmann; **35:** National Archives; **36:** UPI/Bettmann (left), National Archives (right); **37:** Sovfoto/Eastfoto; **38:** Israeli Defense Archives; **39:** UPI/Bettmann (left), Chesnot/Witt/Sipa Press (right); **40:** UPI/Bettmann; **41:** National Archives (left), UPI/Bettmann (right); **42:** Demulder/Sipa Press; **43:** J. Witt/Sipa Press (left), J. Witt/Sipa Press (right)

Contents

The Battle of Waterloo

In a legendary battle, Napoleon was defeated, ending his dream of an empire in Europe.

Napoleon's Rise, Fall, and Return

When the French Republic was collapsing ten years after the 1789 revolution, Napoleon Bonaparte, a successful general, took control of the government. Less than five years later, he crowned himself emperor.

Conquest and Defeat   Not content with ruling France, Napoleon used his army to extend his empire to Italy, Spain, and parts of Germany and Poland. In 1812, he attacked Russia, advancing as far as Moscow before a defeat and a bitter winter forced him to retreat.

Then a new alliance of Great Britain, Russia, and Prussia formed. After months of fighting, they finally beat Napoleon's army. They forced him to leave his throne. In the spring of 1814 he was exiled to the tiny Mediterranean island of Elba. A king from the former French ruling family was put back on the French throne.

The Hundred Days   During Napoleon's exile, diplomats and princes began a meeting called the Congress of Vienna to decide how to reshape Europe. New borders had to be drawn. But more than that was at stake. Napoleon had aroused peoples' desires for their own nations. Many, too, wanted to see the end of domination by kings. The congress was meant to help the kings who had allied against Napoleon reassert their control.

Remembering the achievements of the 1789 revolution, a great many French wanted no part of the king they had been given. Restless on his small island, Napoleon saw his chance to regain power. Less than a year after being sent to Elba, he returned to France. Peasants and troops rallied to him. The king left Paris in a panic. Napoleon formed a new army. But his new regime would last only one hundred days.

Alarmed, the allies in Vienna raised their own armies. British and Prussian troops were already in Belgium. Austrian and Russian soldiers were on the way. Napoleon's only hope was to defeat the force in Belgium before the others arrived. He marched off with 124,000 men.

Final Defeat at Waterloo

The duke of Wellington commanded 94,000 British and Belgian troops. The Prussian army, 123,000 strong, was led by Gebhard von Blücher. To win, Napoleon had to defeat each army before they could join together.

On June 16 he struck the Prussians at Ligny. Another part of his force engaged Wellington. Napoleon pushed the two armies back, but neither was completely beaten. Wellington and Blücher expected the main attack to come at the British next. Wellington made his defensive line on a ridge south of the village of Waterloo. Blücher promised to send reinforcements.

After Ligny, rain struck the area. The British and Prussians moved quickly to implement their plans, but Napoleon was unusually slow. He waited until midday on June 18, 1815, to attack Wellington—he wanted the ground to become as dry as possible. But this delay gave Blücher more time to reach the field.

Napoleon first hit Wellington's line on the right. His goal was to force Wellington to reinforce that

France from the Revolution to Waterloo

1789	National Assembly (legislature) forms new government with less power for king
1792	King Louis XVI imprisoned; republic declared
1793	Louis XVI executed; Reign of Terror begins as enemies of leaders are killed
1794	Terror ends; conservatives take control of government
1799	Napoleon seizes power
1804	Napoleon crowned emperor

area with troops from his center. Then Napoleon would mass the main French attack on that weakened center and break through. But after two hours of fighting, Wellington's right still held.

As he learned of the Prussians' approach, Napoleon gambled. He sent some troops to meet them and launched a furious cannonade against Wellington, then attacked the center. As the French began to break through, a British cavalry charge routed the French infantry. Then a French cavalry counterattack pushed

the British cavalry back. The mounted French then charged Wellington's line many times, facing withering fire. But the line held.

With more Prussians arriving, Napoleon had one last chance: to use his reserves, including the undefeated veterans called the Imperial Guard. But once again he delayed before moving. When he finally ordered the charge, the British and Prussian troops were ready. The French were forced back. Soon after, Napoleon's army and the emperor himself were in an all-out retreat.

Napoleon lost 25,000 dead and wounded and another 8,000 captured. He also lost any last hope of regaining his empire.

Changes in Europe After Waterloo

Forced from his throne again, Napoleon surrendered to the British. They sent him to his final home—another island, called Saint Helena. But this one was not near France, like Elba. Instead, it was far off in the southern Atlantic. Napoleon died there six years later.

Meanwhile the Congress of Vienna finished its work. It restored order after 20 years of war and dashed the hopes of nationalists. Monarchies were restored in France and Spain. Prussia was given land on the Rhine, making it stronger. A new kingdom of the Netherlands was created, with Belgium added to it. Austria was given control of northern Italy again. The new order helped keep peace in Europe for about 50 years.

The most important effect of Waterloo, though, was to end the French effort to control Europe. It would take 100 years before another European power threatened to dominate the continent.

▲ A brilliant general, Napoleon threatened to put all of Europe under French domination.

▼ As French soldiers rally to cover the retreat, a beaten Napoleon prepares to mount his horse and ride away. Within days, he will surrender to the British.

The Battle of Antietam

Following a Union victory on the bloodiest day of the Civil War, President Lincoln issued the Emancipation Proclamation.

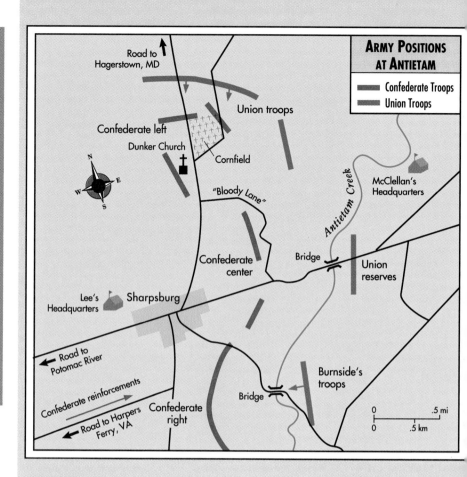

ARMY POSITIONS AT ANTIETAM

Confederate Troops
Union Troops

Road to Hagerstown, MD
Union troops
Confederate left
Dunker Church
Cornfield
"Bloody Lane"
McClellan's Headquarters
Antietam Creek
Confederate center
Bridge
Union reserves
Lee's Headquarters
Sharpsburg
Road to Potomac River
Confederate reinforcements
Road to Harpers Ferry, VA
Confederate right
Burnside's troops
Bridge
0   .5 mi
0   .5 km

McClellan launched a series of attacks that almost broke Confederate lines. Instead of pursuing his advantage, McClellan allowed Lee to retreat to Virginia.

The Early Civil War

Starting in 1861, America was engaged in a terrible Civil War. The country had split over the question of extending black slavery into new western lands. When Abraham Lincoln, who opposed this extension, was elected President in 1860, 13 Southern states seceded from, or left, the United States. They formed a new nation, called the Confederate States of America. The Northern states fought to force the Confederate states back into the Union.

September 1862 was an important month in that war. Both sides needed to win a battle. The South hoped a victory would persuade England and France to give it aid. In the North, Lincoln had decided that the bloody conflict needed a nobler cause than maintaining the Union. He planned to declare the end of slavery in Confederate territory, but he needed a victory before making his announcement.

The Bloodiest Day

The Commanders' Plans   The brilliant Confederate general Robert E. Lee had decided to invade the North to win the needed victory. He slipped north behind a screen of mountains. Then Union general George McClellan had a stroke of luck. A Union soldier found a copy of Lee's orders to his generals. Knowing where Lee was, McClellan made his move.

At Sharpsburg, Maryland, just west of Antietam Creek, Lee positioned his troops. Their line stretched for a mile and a half.

McClellan approached. His army outnumbered Lee's, but McClellan thought Lee's army was larger. That mistake made him cautious.

Still, McClellan had a good plan of attack. Three generals would attack Lee's army on its left, right, and center. Another large force would be held in reserve. It would stay ready to enter the battle to make a final crushing blow.

September 17, 1862   The battle began at dawn. On the left, Union troops moved against Lee's favorite commander, General Stonewall Jackson. The battle raged in a cornfield. Fighting seesawed back and forth as each army charged and countercharged. Within two hours, over 5,000 men were killed or wounded.

Later in the morning, the Union army advanced with new troops, but the Confederates held their line.

Burnside's delay in crossing the bridge on the Confederate right was costly to McClellan, ruining his plan of a coordinated attack. As a result, he was unable to achieve a more decisive victory.

Emancipation Proclaimed

Antietam was not a decisive victory for the North, but it was an important one. Using the news of Confederate general Robert E. Lee's retreat as proof that the North had won the battle, Lincoln issued the Emancipation Proclamation. In it, he freed all the slaves in the territory still controlled by the Confederates. It was not a full measure of freedom for slaves, but it was a sign that war aims had changed. From then on, the North was fighting a war of freedom. It was fighting to create a new United States, not just to preserve the old one.

Antietam also brought loss of confidence in the South abroad. Antislavery and pro-Union sentiment rose in England and France once Lincoln issued the Proclamation. The South lost any possibility of gaining the help it needed to win the war.

Angry with McClellan's caution, Lincoln soon removed him and began a search for a commander who could match wits with Lee.

At Antietam, Lincoln got the Union victory he needed to announce his policy of emancipation of the slaves.

Losses again were massive, but Jackson's troops stood firm.

In the Confederate center, the attack got under way later in the day. The Union troops met fierce resistance in a sunken road. So many troops fell there that it became known as "Bloody Lane." Finally the Southern line in the center was broken; the Union army had a chance to achieve a smashing victory. But McClellan still believed that Lee had a larger army than he. Afraid of a counterattack, he failed to use the reserve troops.

On the Confederate right, the attack was delayed even longer. Union general Ambrose Burnside had to move his troops across a bridge over the Antietam. Southern sharpshooters on the opposite shore kept the Union soldiers from crossing for hours. When they finally did cross in midafternoon, they threatened to overwhelm Lee's army. It was a second chance for the Union to win the battle decisively. But Burnside's men were surprised by Confederate reinforcements and beaten back.

September 18, 1862 The next day, Lee's army held its original position. He was sure that another attack would come. But McClellan again proved reluctant to fight. That night, Lee retreated to Virginia. The invasion had failed. McClellan, however, had failed to smash Lee's army.

The casualties on both sides totaled about 22,000. This was the bloodiest single day of the entire war.

The Three Days of Gettysburg

The Union army defeated a Confederate invasion of the North, ending Confederate hopes of winning the Civil War.

The Civil War Before Gettysburg

The Union army in the Civil War achieved many successes in the West. By the middle of 1863, soldiers there were finally about to capture Vicksburg, the last Confederate stronghold on the Mississippi River.

In the East, the situation was different. Confederate general Robert E. Lee outplanned, outmarched, and outfought a succession of Union commanders. Confident after major victories at Fredericksburg and Chancellorsville, Lee launched his second invasion of the North in June 1863. One of his goals was food. With the South becoming unable to supply his army, Lee aimed to raid Pennsylvania's rich farmlands.

As Lee's army moved north, President Abraham Lincoln named a new army commander. George Gordon Meade, from Pennsylvania, took control of the Union army on June 28, 1863—days before the Battle of Gettysburg began.

Three Bloody Days

General Meade moved north, too. Trying to find Lee, he sent some cavalry and infantry to the small town of Gettysburg, Pennsylvania. Meanwhile a division of Lee's, many barefoot, marched to the same town to get shoes. The two forces met and began fighting on July 1, 1863.

The First Day The troops clashed northwest of the town. As more soldiers from both armies arrived, the fighting became more fierce. In one Union regiment, 80 percent of the soldiers were killed or wounded.

Lee, arriving about noon, ordered a strong attack on the Union soldiers. The Union troops then retired to a strong defensive position on high ground south of town.

The Second Day Meade formed the Union line in the shape of a hook from Culp's Hill to Cemetery Hill and along Cemetery Ridge (see the map).

Lee planned to attack the Union line at three points. General James Longstreet would lead the main attack, against the Union left. Other units would assault the Union right and center. A Union general's error almost won the day for the Confederate side.

Before the Confederates attacked, General Dan Sickles moved his Union soldiers off the ridge to a peach orchard. The foolish move endangered

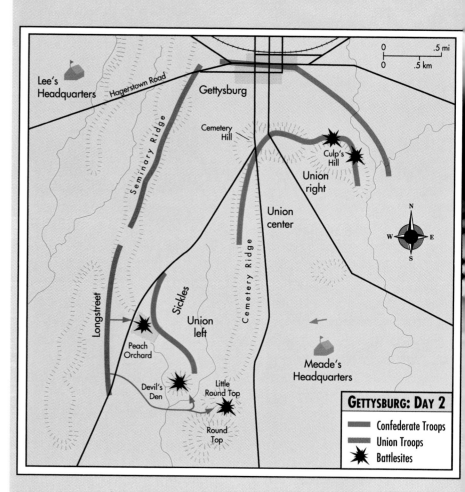

Longstreet's attack on Sickles drove the Union soldiers back to the hills called the Round Tops. If the Confederates had taken that position, they could have shelled the main Union line and won the battle.

his men and weakened the Union position. Longstreet's soldiers smashed into the new line. As the Union soldiers were driven back, the Confederates began to mount the two hills called the Round Tops. From that location, their artillery could shell Meade's soldiers at will.

General Gouverneur Warren saved the Union army. Spotting the oncoming Confederates, he ordered some fresh troops into position. Though fighting raged in the hills and in the rocky area known as Devil's Den, the Union army held firm. Longstreet finally called off the attack. As the day ended, both armies held the same positions as in the morning.

The Third Day Lee decided to attack the Union center. He amassed a force of 15,000 fresh troops and put them under the command of General George Pickett. Pickett had to cross a mile of open space between the armies and cut through the Union line.

Before the charge, the Confederates unleashed a two-hour barrage from over 150 cannons. At first, Union gunners returned fire; then they stopped to save ammunition for the coming attack.

Pickett's army marched across the open ground with flags flying. As they got closer, the Union guns opened fire. The shots ripped holes in the Confederate lines, but the soldiers closed ranks. Union troops moved out of position to fire on the flanks of the attackers. That forced more Confederates into the middle—into the cannon fire. A few hundred actually reached the Union line, but the hand-to-hand fighting was brief. The Confederates had to retreat. On July 4, Lee's army returned to Virginia.

Lee apologized to what remained of Pickett's command. Referring to their terrible losses, he said, "It is all my fault."

After Gettysburg

The battle badly damaged Lee's army, already smaller than the Union force. About 27,000 men were killed, wounded, or captured, 7,000 in Pickett's charge alone. Lee apologized to the remnants of his army.

Meade lost about 23,000 dead, wounded, or captured. But his army had soundly beaten the Confederates. The South got more bad news the day after Gettysburg—Vicksburg had finally surrendered after months of siege. Now the Union controlled the Mississippi. With these two defeats, the South was doomed. It took two more years for the fighting to end, but it was clear that the North would finally win.

That fall, a national cemetery was dedicated at Gettysburg for the dead of both sides. To mark the occasion, President Lincoln gave a short speech—the Gettysburg Address on November 19, 1863. His 271 words have become one of the most memorable speeches in American history.

The fighting at Gettysburg was intense and often at very close range, which sent the number of casualties soaring.

The Battle of Sedan

France's defeat in the Franco-Prussian War signaled Germany's emergence as Europe's greatest power.

France and Germany Opposed

Until the 19th century, what is now Germany was a collection of many separate states. Otto von Bismarck, the chancellor of Prussia—the most powerful German state—changed that. By the late 1860s, his goal of forming a united Germany under Prussian leadership was almost completely achieved. To convince the remaining states to join, he needed a bold move. Bismarck thought that by starting—and winning—a war, he would make the German states fearful for their safety and impressed by Prussian arms. For his target he chose France.

Bismarck's victim was wisely chosen. France's leader was Napoleon III, a weak, self-proclaimed emperor who was the nephew of the great Napoleon. The emperor had begun to lose support. He wanted a war to restore his popularity.

The war came in 1870. After a diplomatic crisis erupted, Napoleon III issued an ultimatum to Prussia. It must apologize for its actions, he said, or there would be war. Bismarck, knowing that the result would favor him, refused. Napoleon III declared war on July 5, 1870.

The Surrender at Sedan

First Moves By late July, the French managed to mobilize two armies, one at Strasbourg and one at Metz. Facing them was a large force of 400,000 soldiers under Field Marshal Helmuth von Moltke.

The French plans were vague. The Prussians had a better idea of what to do. Moltke would use part of his force to hold the French at Strasbourg while the remainder poured into the gap between the French armies and encircled the force at Metz. After destroying that French army, it would take on the other.

Napoleon, who led one French army, won an early skirmish, but by mid-August he had left the field. He was too ill to continue; and besides, Moltke was advancing. The French command was confused. The army at Strasbourg, commanded by Marshal Marie de MacMahon, pulled back toward Paris in the west. Defending Paris from the oncoming Prussians was a logical mission for MacMahon, but the government pressured him to advance. So MacMahon marched northeast. The plan was to unite with the other French army and crush Moltke. Instead, MacMahon led his army into a trap.

The Imperial Guard, like all the French troops, fought bravely at Sedan, but poor generalship led the French into a trap and doomed them to defeat.

The Trap at Sedan Moltke moved swiftly against MacMahon, which surprised the French commander. Dismayed, he changed plans on August 31 and marched away from the other French army, to Sedan. There MacMahon boxed his army into a corner. Trapped in a triangle of land formed by three rivers, he could not quickly move out. Worse, his army was in a valley almost completely surrounded by hills. The Prussians began to take the high ground—a perfect location for placing their artillery. Besides the advantages of terrain, the Prussians outnumbered the French by 90,000. The situation for the French was hopeless.

The actual fighting was brief. General MacMahon tried to break out but could not. Wounded, he passed his command to General Auguste-Alexandre Ducrot. Ducrot recognized the poor prospects for the army and decided to withdraw his troops before the Prussians cut off a line of retreat. Then yet another French general, Emmanuel de Wimpffen, took command. He had orders from the minister of war to fight, and fight he would. Napoleon III was on the scene, but he did not take charge.

By this time, about midday on September 1, Moltke had completely encircled the French army. Prussian cannon fire rained down on the French. The French cavalry tried three times to break the Prussian hold on an escape route. Though hopeless, their charge was heroic. As they retired after the third attack, the Prussian guns stopped firing to honor them. The failed charge convinced the French that they could not escape.

With no outlet and the cannon shells crashing around his army, Napoleon was forced to raise the white flag. On September 2, he surrendered himself and his 104,000 soldiers to Bismarck.

Europe After Sedan

Sedan changed Europe. Two days after the surrender, a people's revolt in Paris brought about a new national government, a republic by the people to replace Napoleon's empire. That republic officially surrendered to the Germans early in 1871. As part of the peace treaty, France had to yield two provinces, Alsace and Lorraine, to Germany.

Germany was the new name of the nation to France's east. Prussia's triumph achieved Bismarck's aims. After his armies occupied Paris, the heads of all the German states met at Versailles. There they proclaimed Wilhelm I—the king of Prussia—emperor of the united Germany. It was now the most powerful nation in western Europe.

The humiliation of Sedan and the loss of Alsace and Lorraine pained the French for decades. Their desire for revenge helped fuel the fierceness of the fighting in World War I. And it helps explain the harshness of the peace treaty that the French demanded of the Germans at the end of that war.

In this watercolor by an artist traveling with the Prussians, the Prussian army advances at night after Sedan. The French were retreating in disarray.

The Prussian army entered Paris through the Arch of Triumph soon after Sedan. The French fought on for another year, but after Sedan, Prussian victory was certain.

The Little Bighorn

The Plains Indians killed an entire U.S. Cavalry command, achieving the last Native American victory in the fight to hold their disappearing land.

Before the Little Bighorn

Mounting Tension By the 1870s, the Native Americans who lived on the Great Plains of the United States were growing desperate. Their land was disappearing as more and more white settlers moved west. Worse, they were losing the buffalo that they needed for food, clothing, and shelter. To clear the way for trains, railroad companies killed the buffalo by the tens of thousands.

The final outrage came in 1874. An expedition found gold in the Black Hills of what is now South Dakota. Fortune-hunting whites rushed to the new strike. The Sioux nation bitterly resented this move. The Black Hills were the sacred home of their gods. A treaty had granted the area to the Sioux in recognition of their traditions. Now white prospectors were being allowed to enter it.

Custer The leader of that 1874 expedition was a cavalry colonel named George Armstrong Custer. Within two years, Custer would play a famous role in the history of Native Americans. Custer was a brave but reckless soldier. After graduating from West Point last in his class, he fought in the Union army in the Civil War and then served in the West.

Custer was flamboyant. When he left West Point, he had his own uniform made—of black velvet. In the West, he wore a buckskin jacket, not the regulation tunic. His long blond hair was a trademark and the source of the Native Americans' name for him—"Long Hair."

The 1876 Campaign The Sioux had left their reservations in protest of the oncoming whites. They gathered, along with members of other tribes, in Montana. They were led by the chiefs Sitting Bull and Crazy Horse. The U.S. Army sent three cavalry columns to attack them and force them to return to the reservations. Custer led part of one of the columns.

On June 17, the Sioux met one of those columns and badly mauled it in a fight. The cavalry returned to its base. The Sioux set up a huge camp near a river called the Little Bighorn.

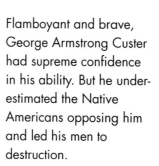

Flamboyant and brave, George Armstrong Custer had supreme confidence in his ability. But he underestimated the Native Americans opposing him and led his men to destruction.

Custer's Last Stand

The U.S. Army command met again to plan its moves. Custer's mission was to search for the Sioux on the Rosebud and Little Bighorn rivers and drive them south. The other forces, moving in from other directions, would trap the Sioux. Before leaving on the mission, Custer refused the offer of extra troops and two Gatling guns (early machine guns). It was a rash decision.

Custer rode his men hard for three days with little rest. Tired, they finally camped for the night early on June 25. The plan was to rest for a day and then seek out the Sioux.

As the troop breakfasted, Custer learned of the huge Sioux encampment. Concerned that he had been spotted and that the Indians would slip away before the other soldiers arrived, he decided to strike. He split his command into four detachments. One was the supply train. The three fighting units were led by Captain Frederick Benteen, Major Marcus Reno, and Custer himself. They went in different directions. Reno and Custer were to attack the Sioux camp from opposite directions while Benteen prevented any Sioux from escaping. Unfortunately, this plan was not based on a thorough scouting of the terrain or the size of the opposing force.

Crazy Horse led the Sioux, who numbered about 3,500. After splitting his command, Custer had 225 troopers with him. Reno's and Benteen's forces were even smaller. The cavalry—especially Custer's unit—was doomed.

Benteen was soon attacked by a group of Sioux fighters. Meanwhile, Reno had reached the camp, and his men had started firing on it. As Custer approached the camp, he ran into a force of about 1,500 warriors led by an able leader named Gall. Custer tried to move his command up to higher ground. But there he was met by Crazy Horse, who had directed another force of 1,500 Sioux around Custer's troops. Together, Gall and Crazy Horse encircled the cavalry. Hemmed in and outnumbered by a vastly superior force, Custer and his troops were all killed.

After the Little Bighorn

While Custer and his 225 officers and men all died, some of Reno's and Benteen's units survived. They had been able to reunite and hold back the attacks on them. When they heard that more soldiers were coming, the Native Americans picked up their camp and moved off.

Although the Sioux were able to smash Custer's command, their cause was hopeless. The settlers kept coming, and so did the army to protect them. The Native Americans had to surrender. Within a year of the Little Bighorn, even so proud a warrior as Crazy Horse had given in and moved to a reservation. But before that year was out he was killed while being arrested—murdered, his people believed.

Sitting Bull took a few thousand followers to Canada. A few years later, starving from decreased supplies of game, they finally gave in. In 1881 Sitting Bull led his last few hundred people to the reservation. In 1890 he was killed in a bungled arrest, as Crazy Horse had been.

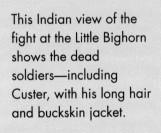

This Indian view of the fight at the Little Bighorn shows the dead soldiers—including Custer, with his long hair and buckskin jacket.

Sitting Bull, shown here, was the spiritual and political leader of the Indians who opposed Custer. But it was Crazy Horse who led the Indians in battle.

The Battle of Tsushima Strait

Japan destroyed
Russian forces in
1905 and emerged as
a world power.

Rivals in the East

World Powers As the 20th century dawned, the great powers of Europe jostled for world domination. Russia, led by Czar Nicholas II, was one of those powers. Even though the country suffered domestic problems and growing popular unrest, the Russian government was more interested in expanding its influence in East Asia. Russia wanted to establish a naval base near its border with China.

Meanwhile, in the Far East, a new power was rising. Japan had been isolated from Europe for centuries. Opened to Western influence only in the 1850s, it had modernized and industrialized quickly. It was now ready to expand and step onto the world stage. Japan, like Russia, looked to China as well as Korea as places where it could grow.

Rival Claims Japan made the first thrust into China, winning a war against the Chinese in 1894–1895. It was ready to seize the Liaotung Peninsula from China. This strip of land on the Asian mainland juts down from Manchuria just to the west of Korea. But Russia, with France's help, blocked Japan's effort and kept China as an area for European expansion. Japan was angered.

The following year, Russia signed a treaty with China. The terms allowed Russia to lease the Liaotung Peninsula to build a naval base and a port. It also permitted Russia to build a railway across northern Manchuria to reach that base. Japan was even more angered. When Russia then began to station troops in northern Korea, the Japanese felt that territory should be under their control and was being taken away. In protest, the Japanese broke off diplomatic relations with Russia on February 6, 1904.

The ships of the Japanese navy were new, heavily armed, and fast.

Some of Russia's ships boasted large guns, but the main fleet was far away in the Baltic, giving the Japanese plenty of time to prepare for a Russian attack.

U.S. President Theodore Roosevelt (*center*) poses with diplomats representing Russia (*left*) and Japan (*right*). Roosevelt helped negotiate the treaty that ended the Russo-Japanese War.

The Russo-Japanese War

Early Moves Two days after ending diplomatic relations, Japan launched a surprise attack against the Russian base at Port Arthur (now called Lüshun) on the Liaotung Peninsula. Two days later, Japan declared war.

In the early fighting, the Japanese proved victorious. They drove Russian land forces out of Korea. In July, they destroyed the eastern fleet of the Russian navy. The Russians decided to send their huge fleet from the Baltic Sea. But it would take months for the ships to round Africa and cross the Indian Ocean.

Meanwhile, the land fighting continued to go Japan's way. In January 1905, Port Arthur fell to a Japanese siege. The next month, the two armies began fighting a huge land battle near the Manchurian city of Mukden (now called Shen-yang). With 624,000 soldiers involved, it was the largest battle in history until that time. Once again, the Japanese beat the Russians decisively.

Tsushima Strait The Russian Baltic fleet set off in October 1904. The commander was Admiral Zinovi Rozhestvenski. Within a week of its departure from the Baltic port of Kronstadt, the fleet almost started a second war. Spotting some British fishing boats at night in the North Sea, the Russians feared that they were small Japanese naval vessels and opened fire. The British were outraged, but Russia's quick apology and the promise of payment prevented further conflict. Meanwhile, with this unlucky beginning, the fleet steamed east. The fleet reached the area in early May 1905. Its seven-month voyage was about to end.

Japanese admiral Heihachiro Togo had his fleet of faster, more heavily armed ships in wait. They lay off the southern coast of Korea, near Pusan. On May 27, they attacked. In two days of fighting, the Russian fleet was destroyed. Fourteen of its 30 ships were sunk, and another 6 were captured. Only 10 ships escaped.

A Changed World

The two combatants were ready for peace. The Russian government had to confront a revolution that had erupted at home. The Japanese, meanwhile, were running out of money to finance the fighting. U.S. President Theodore Roosevelt called diplomats from both sides to peace talks in New Hampshire. As a result of those talks, Russia was forced to give most of its Chinese and Korean territory to Japan.

The defeat showed the weakness of the Russian government, which gave the frustrated Russian people another reason to revolt. Their actions climaxed in a massive general strike in October 1905. During that strike, the first workers' soviets, or councils, were formed. Those soviets would later serve as the core of the Communist Revolution of 1917.

Japan, through its victory, established itself as a world power. It became the first nonwhite nation to defeat a European power. This victory gave heart to nationalists in Iran, Indonesia, Turkey, China, and India, who were trying to throw off the yoke of European colonialism.

15

The Miracle of the Marne

The French and British armies turned back a German invasion, saving Paris and beginning the horrors of trench warfare in World War I.

These French soldiers were also confident of success—and seeking revenge for the devastating loss at Sedan.

When World War I began, these German soldiers marched swiftly and confidently to the front, sure that the war would be brief and victorious.

The First Months of World War I

The War Begins In the early years of the 20th century, Europe was a powder keg waiting to explode. A system of alliances bound Germany and Austria on one side against France, Britain, and Russia on the other. Each side mistrusted the other. Tension also grew because of an arms race that had lasted many decades. When the heir to the Austrian throne was assassinated in Sarajevo, Bosnia, on June 28, 1914, the powder ignited.

Because the assassin was from Serbia, a small European country, Austria declared war on Serbia. Russia, an ally of Serbia, began to mobilize, or prepare its forces for war, against both Austria and Germany. Germany declared war on Russia and its ally France. Germany then launched an attack on France in early August. Its invasion of neutral Belgium caused Britain to declare war on Germany. By early August, most of Europe was at war.

The Generals' Plans After the humiliation of Sedan in 1870, French generals were determined to get revenge. In the years leading up to World War I, they had developed what they thought was a winning strategy. Masses of French soldiers would charge with bayonets fixed to reclaim Alsace and Lorraine, the areas that the Germans had won in the Franco-Prussian War. The plan was long on glory but short on sense. The generals ignored a simple fact. Now that armies had machine guns, this war would be fought differently. Mass infantry attacks would be mass suicide.

The German plan relied on moving troops to attack at the weakest point instead of making a direct assault. An army massed on the French border was to move swiftly through Belgium and head west into France, then turn south. The goal was to get behind the rear of the French armies that would be advancing to the east. After a quick victory, the Germans could turn east to face the Russians.

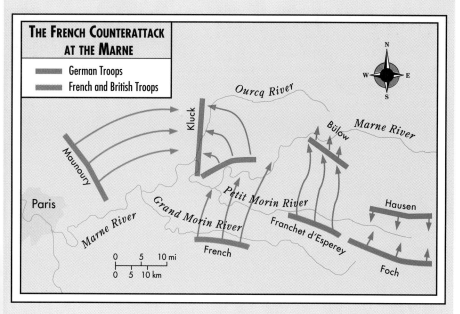

THE FRENCH COUNTERATTACK AT THE MARNE

- German Troops
- French and British Troops

Ourcq River
Kluck
Bülow
Marne River
Maunoury
Paris
Marne River
Grand Morin River
Petit Morin River
Hausen
French
Franchet d'Esperey
Foch
0 5 10 mi
0 5 10 km

Early in the war, three German armies closed on Paris. Maunoury's attack forced Kluck to turn west. This opened a hole between him and Bülow. Now in a poor position, the Germans were forced to retreat.

The First Battle of the Marne

German Success The German advance proceeded largely as planned, stopped only briefly by Belgian resistance. The French attack into Alsace and Lorraine failed. By the end of August, the Germans had moved far into northeastern France, and the French were falling back. A German army, under General Alexander von Kluck, was nearing Paris.

The French Counterattack Two facts gave the French hope. First, a new French force being assembled in Paris threatened Kluck's army. As Kluck kept moving south, he opened himself to attack on his rear. Second, Kluck had become separated from the army in the center, under General Karl von Bülow. The gap in the German line was an opening that the French and their British allies could exploit. The French halted their retreat. French general Joseph Joffre drew up the plan for the counterattack against the German armies near the Marne River.

On September 6, 1914, French general Michel-Joseph Maunoury led the offensive from Paris. Kluck turned to his right to meet the assault. This move widened the gap between him and Bülow. Meanwhile, Bülow was under assault by French general Louis Franchet d'Esperey. Farther to the German left another attack, under General Ferdinand Foch, made little headway but tied up German troops under General Hausen.

The next day saw one of the legendary feats of the war. As the army from Paris faced stiffer opposition, French general Joseph-Simon Gallieni wanted to add more pressure. Seizing about 1,200 Paris taxicabs, he packed them with troops, five soldiers to a cab. The drivers rushed the reinforcements to the front.

The pressure on the Germans was building; their armies were ready to break. Unfortunately, the British army under General John French had advanced too cautiously. French's slowness saved the Germans from annihilation, but their situation was still bad.

On September 9, the German army began its retreat.

Years of Trench Warfare

This battle marked the beginning of trench warfare on the Western Front in World War I. Shortly after the German retreat, the pattern of fighting changed. The armies built elaborate systems of trenches and barbed wire defended by machine guns. For four years, both sides made repeated charges against these stout defenses. Both suffered horrible casualties to gain little ground.

Four years after First Marne, the armies fought over the same terrain. In the Second Battle of the Marne, the Allies—now including Americans—repeated their earlier success. The Germans launched an attack to try to end the war. The Allies met the blow and then counterpunched. This offensive, in the summer of 1918, led the Germans to surrender and ended the horrible slaughter of World War I.

The war continued for four bloody years, with weary soldiers spending much of their time in the boredom of trenches. The high hopes of the early days were gone.

17

The Bombing of Guernica

The world was outraged by the brutal bombing of a village during the Spanish civil war.

Origins of the Spanish Civil War

Political Conflict Turmoil struck Spain in the early 20th century. After centuries of being ruled by a king, Spain saw a movement for democracy arise and, in 1931, triumph. The king left Spain, and a new constitution was approved. But the nation still suffered deep divisions.

Many Spaniards wished to see the new democracy succeed. Called Republicans because they supported the republic, they had allies in more radical parties such as the Socialists and Communists. These groups pushed for major reforms in Spanish society. Conservative Spaniards favored the return of the king. A major group of conservatives belonged to the Fascist Party. They were violently opposed to socialism and communism.

Regional conflicts deepened these divisions. Many ethnic groups in Spain, especially the people of Catalonia and the Basque region, demanded their own government. The conservatives opposed those changes, too.

When the Republicans won elections in 1936, supporters of both sides began to fight in the streets. Chaos loomed.

The Civil War Leaders of the army, opposed to the Republicans' reforms, decided to act. Calling for a revolt against the government in July 1936, they chose General Francisco Franco as their commander and as the head of their government. They called themselves the Nationalists.

The Republicans now renamed themselves the Loyalists (because they were loyal to the republic). They raised an army of their own to fight for their survival.

The war that resulted was especially brutal and attracted international attention. Germany's Adolf Hitler and Italy's Benito Mussolini, both fascist dictators, helped the Nationalists. They even sent troops. The Soviet Union's Communist dictator, Joseph Stalin, sent supplies to the Loyalists. But Britain and France, two major European powers, avoided involvement.

The Attack on Guernica

In the early fighting, neither side gained an advantage. Then, in early 1937, the Nationalists decided to attack Vizcaya, the Basque province in the north of Spain. The Basques were strong Loyalists.

General Emilio Mola led a force of 40,000 troops to conquer the Basque country. Mola made his intentions clear with a threat: "If submission is not immediate, I will raze all Vizcaya to the ground, beginning with the industries of war. I have the means to do so." His "means" included more than infantry. With Mola was the Condor Legion, an air force of bombers and fighters from Germany.

General Francisco Franco (*center*) led the Fascist troops in the Spanish civil war. After his army defeated the Republicans, he became dictator and ruled Spain for nearly 30 years.

Mola wanted to break the spirit of the Basque resistance. On the night of April 25, he met with the commander of the Condor Legion to plan an attack. That night, Mola issued a threatening warning to the Basques: surrender or else.

The next day, the Basque people learned what the alternative to surrender was. On April 26, Mola attacked Guernica, the ancient city that was the traditional center of the Basque region. He chose to attack on market day, when many people were outdoors.

The Condor Legion made the three-hour attack. The Germans first dropped incendiary bombs, meant to burn buildings. Then fighter planes followed to strafe the people. A Basque diplomat described what he saw in the suffering city: "Five minutes did not elapse without the sky's being black with German planes. The planes descended very low, the machine-gun fire tearing up the woods and roads, in whose gutters, huddled together, lay old men, women, and children. . . . Fire enveloped the whole city. Screams of lamentation were heard everywhere."

The attack marked the first time in history that an air assault was used to destroy a city and its civilian population. It also served as an omen of what would come in World War II.

The Legacy of Guernica

World opinion was outraged at the brutal attack. At first the Nationalists denied that they had done anything. They claimed that the Basques themselves had set fire to the city in order to accuse the Nationalists of atrocities. But news reports proved otherwise.

The horror of the attack was vividly displayed by a remarkable work of art. Spanish artist Pablo Picasso, outraged by the bombing, immediately began a painting to commemorate the suffering there. The twisted figures and screaming faces in the finished work clearly show the agony of human suffering caused by war. At a 1937 international exposition, Picasso's painting hung in the pavilion of the Spanish republic for all the world to see.

By 1939, the Nationalists had overthrown the republic, and Franco ruled Spain as a dictator for nearly 30 years. Picasso's painting now hangs in a museum in Madrid, an enduring symbol of the terror of war in the 20th century.

The innocent suffer in Picasso's *Guernica,* a grim depiction of the horror of bombing attacks on civilians. The images on the right and left, of a man trapped in flames and a mother holding the lifeless body of her child, are as compelling today as when they were first painted.

The Taking of Nanking

The Japanese sacked a Chinese city, killing thousands and horrifying the world.

The Japanese named Pu Yi—the last member of the Chinese ruling family—as emperor of Manchuria, but they controlled his actions.

China in Chaos

In the early 20th century, China and Japan were developing in opposite directions.

China had suffered domination by European powers for decades and was beset by chaos. A democratic revolution had overthrown the emperor in 1912, but disorder followed. By the late 1920s, a civil war was raging between two groups. The Nationalists, led by Chiang Kai-shek (now spelled Jiang Jie-shi), wanted to maintain the power of middle class and wealthy people. Opposed to them were the Communists, who wanted to strip the wealthy of their property and give it to the masses of peasants.

Japan was a nation on the rise. Closed to all European contact until the 1850s, it transformed itself thereafter. The government was controlled by business and military leaders. They had developed an industrial economy and built a strong army and navy. Japan sought areas to expand its influence. It eyed China as ripe for the picking.

The War with Japan

Beginnings On the pretext of avenging the murder of a Japanese officer in 1931, Japan invaded Manchuria. It took this area of northern China easily. The Japanese installed Pu Yi, the last surviving Chinese emperor, as a puppet ruler. But he was emperor in name only.

The Chinese appealed to the League of Nations for help. The League charged the Japanese with disturbing the peace, but the weak organization could do nothing to force them out.

For the next few years, little happened in the conflict between China and Japan. The Japanese made occasional inroads into Mongolia but mainly stayed in Manchuria. The Nationalists, meanwhile, continued their civil war against the Communists. In late 1936, however, the two sides agreed to join to fight Japan.

That fight intensified the next year. After an incident in which some shots were fired at Japanese troops near Peking (now called Beijing), Japan launched a full-scale invasion of China. It quickly captured the northern cities of Tientsin (now called Tianjin) and Peking.

The capture of Tientsin signaled things to come: the Japanese looted, burned, and destroyed much of the city. Chinese prisoners were executed, as were the wounded. The purpose was to instill fear and obedience in the Chinese.

The Chinese, too, were cruel. A loosely assembled army of Chinese civilians massacred Japanese in one city. They killed women and children as well as soldiers. But the Japanese were carrying out a determined policy called the "three alls": kill all, burn all, destroy all.

These Japanese troops enter the city of Canton (now called Guangzhou) under the banner of their emperor. As they occupied a new city, the Japanese did not hesitate to kill thousands.

A lonely Chinese baby wails in the midst of a city destroyed by Japanese bombs. Chinese civilians suffered horribly in the war against Japan.

The Destruction of Nanking

Later in the year, the Japanese began moving south. The Chinese fought hard, but the Japanese had stronger forces and continued to press on. By early December, they had surrounded Nanking (now called Nanjing). Bombs fell each day, and thousands of civilians died. As the days went by, the Japanese advanced without being stopped. Finally, on December 13, 1937, they captured the city. One Chinese army group was able to escape, but the rest of the soldiers were captured.

The city that the Japanese entered was a shell of its former self. Buildings had been destroyed by days of bombing. Thousands of Chinese had already died. The conquering army proceeded to make the destruction even more widespread.

They began with mass executions of captured Chinese soldiers. One Japanese regiment reported killing 13,000 prisoners over a few days. But more than soldiers were killed. In a typical incident, about 500 Chinese men were lined up and shot by machine guns. Death followed for many other civilians, including women and children. In all, about 300,000 Chinese were killed in the taking of Nanking.

Along with the killing came looting and burning. Whatever had been left after the bombing was destroyed.

After Nanking

The destruction of Nanking horrified the world. It symbolized the brutality of modern warfare and the growing tendency of armies to kill civilians, including women and children.

After the ruin of Nanking, the Japanese advance continued. By 1938, Japan controlled most of China. Mao Zedong, leader of the Communists, maintained a constant guerrilla war against the Japanese. The Nationalists, however, were reluctant to fight. Even after the United States entered World War II in 1941 and joined with the Chinese to fight the Japanese, the Nationalists had to be forced into battle. Some Nationalists even worked with the Japanese.

These two different responses to the Japanese occupation of China eventually decided China's future. The Chinese people began to support the Communists. By doing so, they helped the Communists win control of China after World War II, when the civil war erupted again.

21

The Battle of Britain

In 1940, British planes beat back a German bombing campaign over Great Britain, ending German hopes of invading the island.

RAF fighter planes were fast and easy to maneuver, making them valuable weapons against the German planes. German aircraft also suffered from being near the end of their flying range.

The Danger to Great Britain

In the summer of 1940, Great Britain's outlook was bleak. German armies occupied most of Europe. They held Austria and Czechoslovakia. They had conquered Poland, Norway, Denmark, Belgium, the Netherlands, and France. Spain and Portugal were neutral but sympathetic to Germany. Italy was Germany's ally. The Soviet Union had agreed not to fight Germany. The United States, though it supplied the British with equipment, had not yet entered the war. Britain stood alone against Germany.

Germany's Adolf Hitler hoped that Britain would simply give up. Then he could focus on his secret aim: to invade the Soviet Union, supposedly an ally. In case Britain didn't surrender, his generals planned an invasion of the island nation. To weaken Britain's defenses, they decided to use the Luftwaffe, or air force, in an intense bombing campaign. The British knew an attack was coming. They just didn't know when it would come.

RAF pilots, warned of approaching German planes by the British radar network, scramble to reach their fighters and engage the oncoming bombers.

Luftwaffe Versus RAF

Facing the Luftwaffe was the Royal Air Force (RAF). The Germans had twice as many planes as the RAF, but their bombers were vulnerable to attack from British fighters. Sir Hugh Dowding, head of the RAF Fighter Command, had a simple plan. He would ignore the German fighters that helped protect the bombers and focus on destroying the bombers.

The British also had a newly installed radar system. Recently invented, radar allowed them to spot oncoming German planes far from their shores. RAF fighters could then meet the attack as early as possible.

Operation Eagle The Luftwaffe began bombing Britain in July 1940. The main attack, called Operation Eagle, was meant to destroy RAF defenses in four days. It began August 13.

The RAF fought brilliantly in those first days. It shot down 256 German planes and damaged many more. The RAF lost 103 planes.

Model	Type of Plane	Abilities
RAF Planes		
Hurricane	Fighter	Easy to fly; durable
Spitfire	Fighter	All metal; easy to maneuver
Luftwaffe Planes		
Dornier	Bomber	Heavily armed; fairly fast
Junker 88	Bomber	Heavily armed
Messerschmitt 109	Fighter	Fast; excellent at climbing
Messerschmitt 110	Two-seat fighter	Long-range; fairly slow

PLANES IN THE BATTLE OF BRITAIN

German planes swoop down on London, already afire from bombs. Radio broadcasts about the attacks on London to the United States helped build sympathy for the beleaguered British.

The Second Phase Frustrated by their heavy losses, the Germans decided to bomb the RAF airfields around the clock.

The RAF was hard pressed by these attacks. As the days wore on, pilots became exhausted. It became harder to replace those who were shot down. But the British held on. Dowding chose not to commit reserve fighters who were hidden in the north.

The Luftwaffe suffered as well. Losses of more than 800 planes and crews in less than two months weakened the German air force and hurt its confidence.

By chance, the battle changed. One night a German bomber strayed over London. Although not ordered to do so, the crew dropped their bombs on the city. Enraged by the attack on civilians, Prime Minister Winston Churchill ordered the RAF to bomb Berlin. This infuriated Hitler, who commanded the Luftwaffe to strike new targets.

The Third Phase On September 7, the planned bombing of British cities began. The Blitz, as it was called, caused fearsome destruction. The first attack on London started huge fires. Civilians huddled in subway stations or basements for safety. The British feared that the invasion would come any day.

On September 15, the Luftwaffe put forth its last great effort. Dowding then decided to use his reserves. He changed tactics, too. His 300 fighters faced 100 bombers and 400 fighters.

At the end of a day of fierce combat, the spirit of the Luftwaffe was broken. The Germans realized that their estimates of RAF losses had been too high. The British still had an effective air force. Bombing continued for months, but there were no more major assaults. With the air war lost, Hitler called off the invasion.

The Battle of Britain cost the Germans over 1,700 planes and 6,000 airmen. The RAF lost 915 planes and 414 pilots. Churchill eloquently stated the debt that the British people owed the RAF pilots. "Never in the field of human conflict was so much owed by so many to so few," he said.

The Battle's Impact

Before World War II, military planners believed that massive bombing could defeat a country. The idea was to destroy a nation's ability to make weapons and to undermine its morale. Although the Luftwaffe didn't succeed in this plan, the lesson was not learned. Huge bombing attacks on cities continued throughout the war. The British and Americans heavily bombed the Germans and Japanese.

Faced with an effective RAF, the Germans moved to a sea strategy in late 1940. They relied on submarines to sink supply ships coming to Britain. Many of these ships sailed from the United States. Although the United States still did not enter the war, its combat ships began to escort the supply convoys.

The biggest effect of the failed assault on Britain took place in Europe. Hitler focused his nation's armies on his chief goal. The German army and air force launched the invasion of the Soviet Union in June 1941.

During the Blitz, Londoners spent many nights in underground air-raid shelters, including subway tubes.

The Battles of El Alamein

British victories in Egypt during World War II preserved Allied control of the Suez Canal and Middle East oil.

Montgomery was Britain's best-known commander in World War II. A good organizer and a bold fighter, he used political skill to get appointed to key commands.

The German Threat in North Africa

By 1940, the German army had captured most of Europe. Italy, a German ally, wanted some success of its own. An Italian army attacked British-held Egypt from its bases in Libya. The British repelled this attack and forced the Italians all the way back to Libya. With his ally threatened, German dictator Adolf Hitler ordered a small tank force under Field Marshal Erwin Rommel to Libya. His orders were to save the port city of Tripoli from the British.

Rommel went beyond those orders, taking the offensive in the spring of 1941. He forced the British to retreat. As his advance continued for a year, he got farther from his supply base in Tripoli. His tanks ran on fuel captured from the British, and his troops used captured trucks.

Still Rommel kept pushing. By June 1942, he was approaching Alexandria, on the delta of the Nile River. If he broke through, he could seize the Suez Canal and cut Britain off from the oil fields in the Middle East.

The Desert Battles

First El Alamein While General Claude Auchinleck arranged the British defenses, panic struck Alexandria. The British embassy staff burned papers and prepared to leave. The British fleet steamed through the Suez Canal to the Red Sea to avoid capture.

Auchinleck tried to stop Rommel at Matruh, but German forces swept around the southern end of the British defenses. The British made their next stand at El Alamein, just 60 miles from Alexandria. A huge area of low land, called the Qattara Depression, lay to the south. Steep cliffs at its edge prevented Rommel from trying to encircle the British army from that direction, as he had done at Matruh. He had to attack head on.

In fighting from July 1 to July 4, Rommel failed to break the British line. Rommel was stopped.

Called "the Desert Fox" because of his clever military tactics in arid North Africa, Rommel frequently disobeyed orders and took chances. In the end, he lost to Montgomery because he couldn't be resupplied.

Alam el Halfa The British and German armies maintained their positions for weeks, digging trenches and laying mines. Prime Minister Winston Churchill replaced Auchinleck with General Bernard Montgomery. The British army got needed reinforcements, including powerful new American tanks. The British now had around 700 tanks; Rommel, who had also been reinforced, had only 443.

Rommel knew that he must attack before the British got even stronger. On August 31, he assaulted the position at Alam el Halfa, at the southern end of the British line. The British held again. Down to one day's supply of fuel, Rommel pulled back.

Second El Alamein Montgomery prepared his own attack. Urged by Churchill to move quickly, he insisted on more time. "If the attack begins in September, it will fail," he wrote. "If we wait until October, I guarantee . . . the destruction of Rommel's army." Churchill agreed.

By late October, after both armies had been reinforced, Montgomery's forces outnumbered Rommel's:

- Montgomery had 195,000 troops, Rommel 104,000.

- Montgomery had 1,200 tanks, Rommel fewer than 500.

- Montgomery had twice the artillery of Rommel and an air force of 1,200 planes.

Rommel could get no further reinforcements; German troops were badly needed for the fighting in the Soviet Union.

On October 23, the attack began. The British infantry was unable to break through Rommel's defenses, however. Montgomery continued to attack for the rest of the month, hitting a different spot in the German line each time. The British couldn't budge the Germans, but Rommel was losing badly needed tanks, and his supplies were being used up.

On November 2, a New Zealand division finally broke through the German line. Rommel knew he had to retreat, but Hitler ordered him to stay. The next night Indian troops pushed Rommel's army out of its last defensive position. Beaten, he ordered a retreat.

North Africa After El Alamein

The victory was a decisive one. It saved the Suez Canal and maintained Allied control of Middle East oil. It pushed the European Axis powers—Germany and Italy—out of Egypt for good. Indeed, it helped expel them from North Africa. Rommel retreated along the North African coast all the way to Tripoli again. Meanwhile, British and American troops landed in Morocco just days after the fighting ended at El Alamein. Rommel now faced armies from two directions.

It took the Allies until May 1943 to completely expel Rommel's army from North Africa. Once they did, the way was prepared for the invasion of Italy. With that invasion, the Allies began the liberation of western Europe.

The British line at El Alamein was perilously near the heart of Egypt and the Suez Canal—an important seaway for maintaining the flow of oil to British armies.

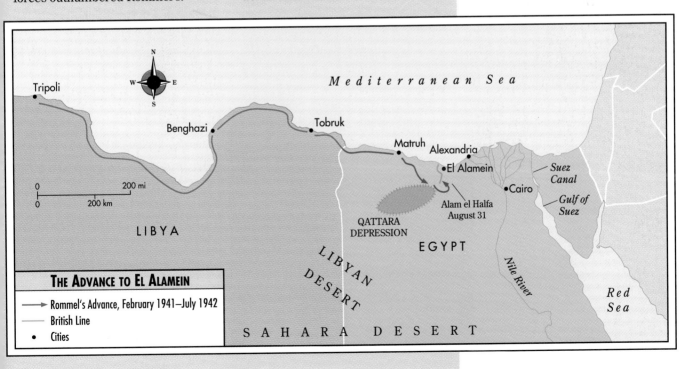

THE ADVANCE TO EL ALAMEIN

→ Rommel's Advance, February 1941–July 1942
— British Line
• Cities

The Battle of Midway

In June 1942, the U.S. Navy destroyed a Japanese fleet, reversing the tide of World War II in the Pacific.

SIZE OF FLEETS AT MIDWAY		
	Japanese*	United States
Aircraft carriers	8	3
Battleships	11	0
Cruisers	22	8
Destroyers	65	15
Submarines	21	0

*Includes ships used in action against Aleutians.

The huge Japanese fleet was actually split into many task forces, some of which were used in the attack on the Aleutian Islands, near Alaska. The key to the U.S. force was its three carriers.

This Japanese print shows the Japanese commander at Midway, Isoroku Yamamoto. He is missing two fingers on his left hand—they were lost at the Battle of Tsushima Strait.

The Early War in the Pacific

Pearl Harbor When World War II opened in the Pacific, the Japanese made quick gains. They took small island outposts named Guam and Wake. They captured Thailand and Burma, including the British fortress at Singapore. They conquered the Philippines as well. The Japanese seemed unstoppable.

The Japanese launched their attack on the U.S. Navy base at Pearl Harbor, Hawaii, on December 7, 1941. They badly damaged the Pacific Fleet. But the Japanese made two mistakes. First, they did not completely destroy the base's repair facilities and oil storage tanks. Thus it could still function. Second, they did not seek out the American aircraft carriers, which had not been at Pearl Harbor. With its carriers intact, the United States could strike back.

The first blow came in April 1942. Sixteen bombers launched from the deck of an American carrier bombed Tokyo. The Japanese command was shocked. Then a U.S. force led by two carriers won a victory at the Battle of the Coral Sea.

New Strategy To win the war, Japanese admiral Isoroku Yamamoto knew, he had to destroy the American carriers. He assembled a huge fleet (see the table) split into eight groups. Four groups would mount a small attack at the Aleutian Islands just off Alaska. At the same time, four larger groups would head to Midway Island. Almost 1,200 miles northwest of Hawaii, Midway was an airfield and lookout post. The heart of this attack force was four large carriers. When the U.S. fleet came north to save the Aleutians, the Japanese ships would destroy them.

Fortunately for the United States, the U.S. Navy knew of Yamamoto's plans. Intelligence officers had cracked the Japanese code. Admiral Chester Nimitz assembled a small fleet of three carriers. One was the *Yorktown,* damaged during the Coral Sea battle. Seventy-two hours of round-the-clock repairs at Pearl Harbor made it seaworthy. The American force steamed to Midway, to hide northeast of the island.

The Fight at Midway

The Battle of Midway was brief but decisive. Japanese planes left their carriers' decks at dawn on June 4, 1942, to bomb Midway. But their main target—the U.S. bombers based on the island—was not hit. Knowing of the attack, the Americans had launched these planes to strike the Japanese fleet. They caused no damage, however.

While the Japanese prepared a second wave of planes to attack Midway, they got a surprise. A Japanese scout plane radioed news of the presence of the U.S. ships. Admiral Chuichi Nagumo, in charge of the carriers, ordered a change in his planes' armament. The bombers should be fitted with torpedoes instead of bombs so they could attack the ships. Then confusion struck. The scout plane reported that the U.S. fleet had no carriers. Half an hour later, it confirmed the presence of carriers. With each report, Nagumo ordered his crews to refit the planes—first for bombs again (to attack the island) and then once more for torpedoes (to attack the carriers). The changes cost the Japanese valuable time.

Then dive bombers from the American carriers struck. The first wave failed; 35 of 61 planes were shot down by Japanese fighters and anti-aircraft fire. But a second group got through. Within minutes their bombs struck three of the four Japanese carriers, including Nagumo's ship. Explosion after explosion racked the decks. Fires burned everywhere. Listing decks spilled burning planes into the sea.

The last of the Japanese carriers launched two flights that badly damaged the *Yorktown*. The American captain ordered his men to abandon ship. But a scout plane from the *Yorktown* spotted the last Japanese carrier. It radioed the location to the U.S. fleet. A last group of bombers arrived to sink the fourth Japanese carrier.

Knowing that he had no air power left to combat the American fleet, Yamamoto broke off the attack in the early hours of June 5. His four large carriers had been destroyed in one afternoon, three of them within minutes of each other.

The Aftermath of Midway

The action at Midway ended on June 7. The *Yorktown,* being towed back to Pearl Harbor, was finally sunk by a Japanese submarine. The U.S. Navy lost one carrier, one destroyer, and about 150 planes in the battle. The Japanese fleet, however, lost four prime aircraft carriers and over 300 planes and pilots.

The Battle of Midway was a huge blow to Japanese plans—and pride. Japan's defeat there marked the end of Japanese advances in the Pacific. Pearl Harbor could no longer be threatened, and the West Coast of the United States was safe. The Japanese still held vast stretches of the Pacific by the end of 1942. Three years of bitter fighting still remained. But the tide had turned.

At a key point in the battle, U.S. planes leave three Japanese aircraft carriers in flames. With his carriers sunk, Yamamoto was forced to withdraw.

The Stalingrad Campaign

The six-month battle in World War II ended German hopes to conquer the Soviet Union.

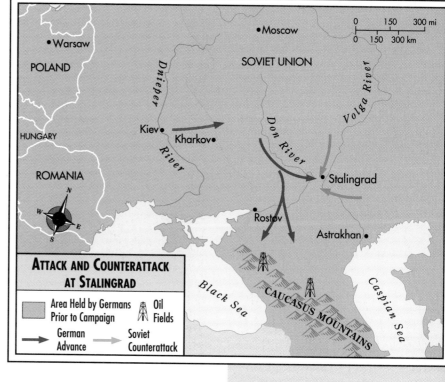

ATTACK AND COUNTERATTACK AT STALINGRAD

Area Held by Germans Prior to Campaign

Oil Fields

German Advance

Soviet Counterattack

World War II Before Stalingrad

Adolf Hitler, who became chancellor of Germany in 1933, dreamed of creating a German empire in Europe. He hoped, in the process, to rid this empire of Communists and Jews, groups he despised. He knew that he could meet his goals only by fighting. But if France, Great Britain, and the Soviet Union joined together, Germany would have to fight on two fronts.

The Early War   To solve his problem, Hitler made an alliance with the dictator of the Soviet Union, Joseph Stalin. Then, in 1939, Hitler launched World War II by invading Poland. His army quickly conquered the country. The next year he turned west and soon took Belgium, the Netherlands, and France.

Germany's defeat in the Battle of Britain spared the island from invasion. Deciding to ignore Britain for a while—as well as his alliance with Stalin—Hitler took aim at the Soviet Union.

The Invasion of the Soviet Union

The Germans invaded the Soviet Union on June 22, 1941. They attacked with 153 divisions—three-quarters of their army. German allies—Romania, Finland, Hungary, and Italy—supplied 30 more divisions.

The initial advance on three fronts—toward Leningrad in the north, Moscow in the center, and Rostov in the south—made stunning progress. German tanks and soldiers smashed through Soviet lines. Hundreds of thousands of the Soviet Union's Red Army soldiers were killed or surrendered.

Stalin took counteraction:

- He took factories apart and rebuilt them behind the safety of the Ural Mountains.

- He ordered his soldiers to burn anything left in retreat, so the Germans could gain no food or fuel.

- He assembled new armies.

By the end of 1941, the Germans had taken vast amounts of land and badly hurt the Soviet army.

The German offensive in the southern Soviet Union captured Stalingrad but it took longer than expected. Hitler's order to send part of the army south weakened the German advance. Three months later the Soviet army counterattacked.

Stalingrad: Plan Blue

The main German thrust in 1942, called Plan Blue, was aimed at the south. The army was to seize Stalingrad and then move farther south to seize oil fields between the Black and Caspian seas.

The German Attack   Starting on July 28, the Germans quickly pushed ahead. Then Hitler gave an order that hurt his chances of success. Thinking that the Soviet defensives were collapsing, Hitler split the German army and ordered one part toward the oil fields. Thus a smaller force than planned attacked Stalingrad.

General Friedrich Paulus's army reached Stalingrad by August 23. The Soviet troops fought hard. The

Soviet troops scramble over rubble to reach another building in Stalingrad, where fierce fighting went from house to house.

When the German army surrendered, the sorry condition of its soldiers became clear—with few coats, blankets, and boots, they suffered terribly from the cold.

German advance was no longer measured by scores of miles, but by city blocks—even houses. The Germans needed two and a half months to capture the city.

The Soviet Counterattack Soviet general Georgi Zhukov now faced Paulus. Massing two fresh armies northwest of the city, he smashed through surprised troops there on November 18. Another Soviet army moved around the city from the south. Paulus was surrounded.

The Germans needed food, fuel, and ammunition. With the bitter Russian winter coming, they needed warm clothes too. Supplies were sent in by air.

Hitler ordered Paulus to stand fast while a relief column under General Hermann Hoth tried to break through the Soviet army. By mid-November, Hoth was only 30 miles away from the city. Paulus then made a mistake. Obeying Hitler's orders to stand, he waited rather than fighting his way out to join Hoth. When Zhukov's army forced Hoth to break off the attack, Paulus was doomed.

For the next two months Zhukov slowly drove in on the Germans in Stalingrad. The Soviets took the airport in mid-January, ending flights that brought supplies in and casualties out. The German soldiers were frozen, with little ammunition, and hungry. The Soviet troops continued their advance. Finally even Paulus was captured. On February 3, 1943, the last Germans surrendered.

The Eastern War After Stalingrad

The city of Stalingrad was largely destroyed by the long fighting. Few buildings remained.

Also destroyed was Paulus's army. The Germans lost almost 150,000 dead in the Stalingrad fighting; 91,000 more became prisoners. The Red Army also suffered. Almost 50,000 Soviet troops died in the last stages of the battle alone.

German hopes to conquer the Soviet Union died in Stalingrad, too. In the summer of 1943, the Soviets began their own offensive. Over the next two years, they pushed the Germans all the way back to Berlin. This advance played a decisive role in Hitler's defeat and, as a result, allowed the Soviet Union to gain control of much of Eastern Europe and emerge from World War II as a military superpower.

The Normandy Invasion

The landing of Allied forces in France marked the beginning of Hitler's defeat in World War II.

Planning the Invasion

In 1944, Germany occupied nearly all of Europe. After two years of fighting in North Africa and Italy, the Americans and British planned to attack the German defenses in France. The Soviet Union, an ally, had wanted such an attack for years to force the Germans to fight on two fronts.

Eisenhower was greatly admired for the skillful way he handled D-Day, the largest amphibious landing ever attempted.

The invading troops would meet strong defenses. "Fortress Europe," German leader Adolf Hitler called it. His armies covered the French coast with concrete bunkers that held artillery and machine guns. They also laid mines and erected barriers to landing craft.

Under American general Dwight D. Eisenhower, the Allies assembled a colossal force in Britain to attack that fortress. This army included American, British, and Canadian troops plus soldiers from France, Poland, and other countries occupied by Hitler. It took 18 months to plan the invasion. The Allies had to assemble a massive army of planes, ships, men, tanks, artillery, and supplies. The force included:

- 1,200 fighting ships
- 804 transport ships
- 10,000 planes
- 4,126 landing craft
- 132,500 troops to land on the beaches
- 23,500 paratroops to land behind enemy lines

The Allies built two artificial harbors that were stored in pieces to be brought to the French landing site once the area had been cleared of German troops.

Plans were drawn up for a highly coordinated attack. Ships and planes would bombard the coastal defenses. Paratroops would land to seize key crossroads. Infantry would assault five beaches.

Finally everything was ready. Operation Overlord, as it was called, could begin. Everyone in Europe knew that an invasion was coming. The question was where.

The massive Allied invasion force moved from many bases throughout southern England to strike the Normandy beaches.

NORMANDY: OPERATION OVERLORD

- Allied Area
- German-occupied Area
- Area Held by Allies by June 7
- Area Held by Allies by June 25
- Allied Invasion Route, June 6
- Allied Paratroop Landing, June 6
- City or Town

The invasion plan called for ships to bombard the German defenses from offshore. Then the infantry had to cross the remaining water in landing craft to reach the beach.

Operation Overlord

The Germans believed that the Allies would invade at Calais, where the English Channel was most narrow (see map). But Eisenhower chose Normandy. The nearby port of Cherbourg would help the Allies land equipment after they moved off the beaches.

Delay and Go The invasion was scheduled to start on June 5, 1944. Then bad weather struck. As rain poured onto the soldiers waiting on the ships, Eisenhower postponed the move. The next night, as the storm lessened, Overlord was launched.

As the fleet of ships left England, thousands of planes took off. Many bombed German defenses. Others took paratroopers behind German lines. Their goal was to prevent the Germans from reinforcing the soldiers defending the beaches.

Five Beaches The five areas chosen for landing each had its own name:

- Americans were to land at Omaha and Utah.

- The British and Canadians were assigned Gold, Juno, and Sword.

To ease the way, thousands of ships opened fire on Fortress Europe. But the naval bombardment couldn't destroy the fortress. Soldiers had to finish the job.

The British at Gold and Sword were able to move off the beaches quickly. Success at Gold cleared the way for one of the artificial harbors. Now the Allies could land heavy vehicles and supplies. The landing at Juno was initially held up by rough seas but later made good progress. By the end of the day, the British had neared Caen, a crossroads city.

Americans at Utah moved rapidly as well. The force landed a bit off target and met little resistance. At Omaha, though, the story was different. Rough seas prevented the planned landing of tanks. Further, the terrain was worse at Omaha, and the German troops there were among the enemy's toughest fighters. The American soldiers were pinned on the beach for hours. Finally, though, they broke through.

The Aftermath

By the end of the first day, the British and Canadians had moved two to three miles inland. Within four days, the Germans were driven back. Still, Cherbourg was not taken until June 27 and Caen not until July 18. With the capture of Saint-Lô on July 25, the Allies finally had their breakthrough. They drove the Germans out of France, liberating Paris on August 25 and then reaching the eastern border of France by the end of the year.

In the aftermath of Normandy, some German generals felt that only by removing Hitler could their country be saved. They tried to assassinate him, but the plot failed. Hitler removed a number of generals from their commands and even had several of them executed.

Coupled with Soviet advances to the east, the Normandy invasion marked the beginning of the end for Hitler. Within a year of the invasion, Germany had surrendered and Hitler had committed suicide.

The Chinese Civil War

Chinese revolutionaries created a Communist government in the world's most populous country.

These peasant soldiers, armed only with lances, marched with Mao Zedong's Communists. Mao's success in winning the peasants' support helped him defeat the Nationalists.

Origins of the Civil War

In 1911, a democratic revolution took place in China. The emperor was forced to resign in early 1912. Soon the country fell into chaos that lasted for years. In northern China, various warlords controlled large regions. An alliance of two groups led the government. The Nationalists wanted to maintain the new democratic government and the power of the middle class and wealthy. The Communists wanted to radically change Chinese society by giving property to the poor.

In 1928, the government finally drove the warlords from the north. Then the Nationalists turned against the Communists and began a civil war against them.

At the same time, China was beset by Japan. Seeing the confusion in China, the Japanese sensed a chance to increase their influence. In 1931, they took all of Manchuria in northern China.

Despite these moves, the Nationalists, led by Chiang Kai-shek (Jiang Jie-shi), were more concerned with defeating the Communists. In 1934, they forced the Communists, under Mao Zedong's leadership, to flee to northern China. This escape, called the Long March, took more than a year. Almost 100,000 Communists began the trip; only about 10,000 finished it.

Many Chinese resented the Nationalist strategy. They wanted to fight the Japanese. When Chiang Kai-shek went to northern China in 1936 to launch a final campaign against Mao, two generals seized Chiang and held him until he agreed to end the civil war. The Nationalists and Communists formed an uneasy alliance.

The next year the Japanese launched a major offensive and captured northern China. Then the pace of the war slowed.

The two Chinese groups handled the conflict with Japan differently. Mao's Communists conducted a guerrilla campaign. They harassed Japanese troops. The Nationalists fought little. They were content to give up land in the hope of buying time. When the United States entered World War II in 1941, the Japanese had a major war on their hands.

The Communist Triumph

When Japan surrendered to end World War II, both Nationalists and Communists renewed their struggle for control of China.

The United States forged a truce between the two sides, but it lasted only a few months. The Nationalists launched a major offensive in June 1946, attacking the Communists in northern China. Trying to preserve their forces, the Communists pulled back. They fought a guerrilla war.

Meanwhile the Communists began a political offensive. They won support of peasants by passing a land reform law in areas they held that allowed poor farmers to own land. The Communists were also helped by unrest in Nationalist areas. Students and workers staged protests against Nationalist brutality, corruption, and cooperation with the Japanese.

After the civil war, Mao created a government that exercised tight control over the Chinese people. Even today, many Chinese are still trying to get more freedom and democracy in their huge nation.

Two Chinas

The Nationalists set up their own government in Taiwan, vowing to return. The United States supported them for years, not even recognizing the Communists as the legal government of mainland China. That changed in 1972, when President Richard Nixon opened diplomatic relations with the Communist Chinese.

In the years that followed 1949, the Communists, under Mao Zedong, cemented their control of the nation. They were the first Chinese government in over 100 years to control all of mainland China. China was modernized and industrialized. But the Communists maintained an iron grip on the people. Even as recently as 1988, when it seemed that a movement for greater freedom would succeed in China, the government cracked down on dissenters.

Taiwan has become one of the success stories of the modern economic world. Its people have prospered. But the two Chinas are still bitter opponents.

In 1947, the Communists began a series of military strikes. They had fewer troops than the Nationalists—one million to four million. As a result, they decided to concentrate on individual Nationalist armies and defeat them one at a time.

The Communists won major victories in the north. As they succeeded, their ranks grew. By the summer of 1948 they had almost 3 million men under arms compared to the Nationalists' 3.5 million. That year was a major turning point. The Communists won major victories in Manchuria and at the Battle of Huai-hai. Other successes came at Kalgan and Tientsin (now called Tianjin). Time was running out for the Nationalists.

Early in 1949 the Communists won the ancient capital, Peking (now called Beijing). The general defending it surrendered his garrison of 250,000 soldiers. The Nationalists grew desperate. In the cities they still held, they rounded up people suspected of Communist sympathies and had them shot.

Province after province fell under Communist control. In the second half of 1949, the Communists defeated nearly two million Nationalist troops in various battles. At the end of that year, the Nationalist government fled to the island of Taiwan. A new regime would now rule mainland China.

The other China, founded by the Nationalists on the island of Taiwan, is now a prosperous nation. But Taiwan's people are not completely free, either.

The Inchon Campaign

A daring landing during the Korean War saved the South Korean government but resulted in the Chinese Communists entering the war.

The Outbreak of War in Korea

After World War II, Communist governments and the Western democracies opposed each other in a conflict called the Cold War. The two sides struggled for control of other countries, but their armies did not fight. In 1950, the Cold War turned hot.

Korea was a divided nation. The Communists controlled North Korea. The United States supported the government of South Korea. Since both parts wanted to control the entire country, a war was bound to come.

On June 25, 1950, North Korea invaded the South. Led by the United States, the United Nations passed a resolution condemning the action. The UN also approved the formation of an army to fight the North Koreans. But while that army from many nations—the Allies—began to assemble, the North Koreans kept pushing the South Koreans back. By August, the North Korean army confronted the Allies, who only held a small pocket around Pusan.

The Inchon Campaign

The Plan Meanwhile, the Allies were planning a counterattack. Commanding all the Allied troops was American general Douglas MacArthur, a hero of World War II. MacArthur decided to both strike behind the North Korean lines and attack the North Koreans at Pusan.

The North Koreans had supply problems. All supplies to the North Koreans attacking near Pusan had to funnel through the South Korean capital, Seoul. By attacking at this point, MacArthur hoped to cut off the North Koreans' supplies. The attack from Pusan would then drive the North Koreans out of the South.

Invasion Seoul is 20 miles inland. To reach it, the army had to land first at the port city of Inchon. The landing site was not ideal. Many islands, strong currents, and 30-foot tides made a landing difficult.

In the end, the operation went more smoothly than could be hoped. The North Koreans had only about a thousand troops in Inchon and only a few thousand more in Seoul. Five days of air bombardment and shelling by ships weakened their defenses. When the U.S. Marines landed on an island in the harbor on September 15, they took it quickly. Then they landed on the mainland the next day and were able to secure the city in a few days.

Breakout at Pusan The second part of MacArthur's strategy was to break the North Korean line at Pusan. On September 16, the day after the Inchon invasion was launched, this counterattack began. About 150,000 United Nations troops, mostly Americans and South Koreans, moved forward. Facing them were 70,000 North Koreans, tired by the weeks of fighting. In the North Korean army were South Koreans

MacArthur, shown here in his trademark leather jacket, had to convince his superiors to accept his bold plan to invade at Inchon.

who had been enlisted by force. They did not wish to fight, but the North Koreans threatened to kill them if they did not.

The attack by UN troops broke through the North Korean lines as planned. The Allied army had far more firepower than the North Koreans could manage. Airplanes struck the North Koreans with bombs, machine-gun fire, and napalm, a petroleum-based jelly that burns. Within days the North Koreans were retreating and thousands surrendered.

The advance was rapid. By September 25, the Allied armies from Inchon and Pusan had linked near the city of Seoul. The fighting near Seoul was fierce. One U.S. Marine company saw 176 of its 206 soldiers killed or wounded. It took a few more days to clear the capital of the North Koreans, but the task was finally completed.

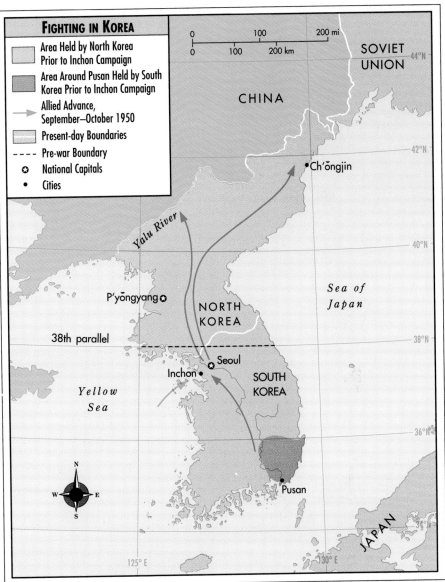

After the invasion at Inchon and the breakout at Pusan, the United Nations forces advanced rapidly to the Yalu River. But when the Chinese entered the war to aid the North Koreans, they regained lost North Korean territory.

Korean refugees flee from fighting that ravages their homes, a familiar sight throughout the 20th century.

China Enters the War

The Allies continued their rapid advance, invading North Korea in early October. Eventually they neared the border of Communist China. The Chinese warned them to stop, but MacArthur pressed the attack. In late October, the Chinese entered the war. The fresh troops drove the Allies back. By January 4, 1951, the Communists held Seoul once again.

MacArthur had wanted to expand the fighting into China. U.S. President Harry Truman, fearing that such an act would start another world war, refused to permit it. When MacArthur urged his position publicly, Truman fired the general.

The Allies eventually fought their way back to the border between North and South Korea, where the war continued for two more years. The fighting ended when the two sides agreed to a truce in July 1953. Korea remained two nations, which it still is today.

The Siege of Dien Bien Phu

Vietnamese forces surrounded and defeated a French army, ending French control of Vietnam.

▼ Ho Chi Minh led the people of Vietnam to independence from the French. But fighting continued in that troubled land for many years after the victory over the French.

France Versus Vietnam

As World War II ended, the peoples of French Indochina wanted independence. The French offered to grant Cambodia, Laos, and Vietnam self-rule but with some form of continuing French control. Cambodia and Laos agreed. But the leader of Vietnamese independence, Ho Chi Minh, refused. War broke out in 1946.

Ho fought the French with the Vietminh, the same army he had led against the Japanese during the 1940s. He used the same guerrilla tactics, too. His troops struck the French with small units and then quickly slipped away. Ho asked the United States for aid, but the request was refused because Ho was a Communist. The United States feared the growing power of communism. That fear grew in 1949, when China, the world's most populous nation, came under the control of a Communist leader. Instead, the United States gave aid to France, its ally. By 1952 the United States was supplying 40 percent of the cost of the war.

The war lasted years. Commanding the Vietminh was General Vo Nguyen Giap. The French wanted to destroy Giap's ability to strike wherever he wanted. But they lacked the troops to cover the entire country. At the beginning, the French had superior weaponry. But as time went on, the Vietnamese got better weapons from the Soviet Union and Communist China. With more soldiers, equally powerful weapons, and a strong urge to win, the Vietnamese had the advantage.

In 1953, the French hit on a new strategy. They would drop soldiers by parachute at strategic spots to seize Giap's supplies. When two such operations succeeded, the French planned another. The target was a village named Dien Bien Phu.

▶ The French plan called for using air drops to supply Dien Bien Phu. But Giap's artillery soon made it too dangerous for the French to fly.

Vietnamese soldiers celebrate over a fallen French plane. The Geneva peace talks gave them an even greater cause for celebration—independence.

The Long Siege of Dien Bien Phu

Operation Castor The plan, called Operation Castor, was bold. The French would drop a strong force of paratroopers in the valley of Dien Bien Phu, in the midst of country controlled by Ho. The size of the French force would compel the Vietminh to fight there—and ensure a French victory.

The first troops landed in late November 1953. By the time the base was completed, the French had 15,000 troops, 60 artillery pieces, and 10 tanks. The soldiers were positioned in a valley surrounded by hills. They controlled an airstrip, which could be used to land supplies.

Meanwhile, Giap was preparing his attack—one that would surprise the French. He had a larger army than the French thought he had. He also had about 200 artillery pieces.

The Siege On March 13, 1954, Giap opened fire. The French were stunned by the ferocity of the bombardment. Within five days, the Vietminh had captured three of the hills surrounding the garrison. They had also destroyed the airfield, forcing

the French to drop supplies to the garrison by parachute. But since Giap had 180 antiaircraft guns in the hills, that was a dangerous method. The Vietminh shot down over 60 planes and helicopters during the weeks of battle.

For the next ten days, Giap bombarded the French. Starting on March 30, he launched massive infantry attacks. The Vietminh suffered heavy casualties, but they drove the French back into a smaller and smaller area. Fierce fighting continued during April.

By May, the situation was hopeless. The French asked the United States to bomb the Vietminh positions. They even suggested using atomic bombs. The United States refused. Meanwhile, Giap closed in. He had 50,000 soldiers now; the French had only 11,000. They had food for only three days and very little ammunition left.

Giap launched his final attack on May 1. Again and again his soldiers charged, taking more French positions. On May 6, Giap slammed the garrison with rockets fired from Soviet rocket launchers. The next day the French surrendered.

The Independence of Vietnam

Giap's timing was superb. An international conference in Geneva, Switzerland, was to discuss French Indochina on May 8. After announcing the surrender at Dien Bien Phu, the Vietminh could negotiate from strength.

In the final agreement, France recognized Vietnam as independent. The country was temporarily divided into northern and southern areas. National elections were scheduled for 1956, at which time the two parts were to unite.

The United States was not upset by the French loss of a colony. But it was alarmed by the arrival of another Communist government in Asia. The United States began to support the non-Communist government of South Vietnam. In 1956 the United States canceled the election in the South. Soon U.S. advisers were helping the South Vietnamese army fight a war against the North. Eventually the U.S. government sent American troops to fight in Vietnam in an unsuccessful war that bitterly divided the American people.

The Six-Day War

Israel defeated its Arab neighbors and seized their land in a stunning victory.

The Birth of Israel

After the Nazi German butchery of Jewish people during World War II, many Jews renewed their demands for a Jewish nation. Finally, in 1947, the United Nations agreed to divide Palestine into Jewish and Arab sections. The Arabs resented the decision, feeling that their land was being taken away. Tension broke into open conflict. Arabs raided the Jewish sector; Jews formed fighting groups to resist.

In 1948, the Jews in Palestine declared the existence of a new nation—Israel. War erupted between this new nation and its Arab neighbors. Israel won that war, ensuring its survival—at least for a while—and increasing its territory. The conflict left about half a million Palestinians without their own country. Arab nations refused to take them in.

In 1956, war broke out again. Israel fought Egypt over access to the Suez Canal. It won the battle, but Egypt continued to bar Israeli ships from using the canal.

A Swift Victory

The Rise of Tension in 1967 Surrounded by Arab countries that vowed to destroy it, Israel always feared for its safety. A United Nations force patrolled the Sinai Peninsula to its southwest, but danger was ever present. Then, in May 1967, Egyptian president Gamal Abdel Nasser ordered the UN troops out of the Sinai. He then blockaded Israel's lone southern port, Aqaba. Israel and the Arab nations put their troops on alert. They traded artillery fire. On June 3, the Israeli government decided to attack, to prevent the Arabs from attacking first.

The Fighting Israel had three opponents—Egypt to the southwest, Jordan to the east, and Syria to the northeast. In just six days, Israel decisively beat each force.

The first day, June 5, began with air assaults. Israel attacked Egypt in the morning, Jordan and Syria in the afternoon. Most Arab planes were destroyed on the ground. In all, the Arab states lost almost 400 planes; Israel lost only 18. After that day, Israel controlled the skies.

The Israelis began their ground attack on the first day as well. Striking the Egyptians, they met resistance but pushed ahead. The Egyptians' lack of air support made the difference. Bombed by Israeli planes that flew unchallenged, the Egyptians began to retreat on the second day.

▶ Israeli pilots effectively won the Six-Day War when they destroyed the air forces of Egypt, Jordan, and Syria on the first day. The move allowed Israel to control the skies.

▼ Outnumbered by its Arab opponents, Israel evened the odds by striking first and striking quickly.

STRENGTH OF ARMIES BEFORE SIX-DAY WAR

Country	Soldiers	Tanks	Planes
Egypt	280,000	1,400	550
Jordan	68,000	250	80
Syria	104,000	600	150
Total	452,000	2,250	780
Israel	289,000	800	350

On the fourth day, the Israelis advanced all the way to the Suez Canal. After a huge battle of about 1,000 tanks, Israel forced the Egyptians to leave the Sinai.

Israeli troops began their move against Jordan on the second day. By the third day, they had sent the Jordanian army back across the Jordan River. The Israelis seized the area now called the West Bank and joyfully marched into the ancient Hebrew capital, Jerusalem.

The fighting against Syria took place on the fifth and sixth days. Air strikes, artillery fire, and tanks allowed Israeli infantry to seize the Golan Heights. Syria had used this high ground to position artillery to bombard Israel. Once the Golan was captured, such shelling was no longer possible.

Israeli soldiers celebrate after occupying Jerusalem, the ancient capital of the Jewish people. Because the city is also a holy place to Muslims, Israeli possession of Jerusalem remains an obstacle to peace.

The Palestinian Problem

Israel's success was stunning. With fewer than 3,500 killed and wounded, it had destroyed 400 planes and about 1,000 tanks and seized land that almost doubled its size.

But Israel's future was still clouded. The Arabs, more resentful than ever, vowed revenge. Also, in seizing the West Bank, Israel acquired about 1.3 million Palestinian Arabs who lived there. They now lived within Israel's borders but did not have full political rights. Still more Palestinians were refugees. Forced to live in other Arab lands, they desperately wanted their homeland back. Their hopes dimmed as Israelis began to settle in the West Bank in large numbers. More than 25 years after the Six-Day War, the problem of a homeland for the Palestinians still remained an obstacle to finding a permanent peace.

Fighting continued for years.

- Palestinian terrorists launched many attacks against Israel. The Israeli army responded with its own attacks on the terrorists or on refugee camps suspected of harboring terrorists.
- Another war broke out in 1973. Israel again won, though much less easily.
- Fighting broke out in Lebanon. That nation was almost destroyed by a civil war in which Palestinian refugees were a factor.
- Starting in 1987, the Palestinians in Israel began a long and bloody revolt to protest their lack of a homeland.

Still, there were some signs that peace might finally come. Israel and Egypt signed a treaty in 1979, and Israel pulled out of the Sinai. And in 1991, after the Persian Gulf War, Israel and the Arab nations finally began talking peace to each other. Many problems remained to be solved in these peace talks, but the world was hopeful that the nations would reach a lasting peace agreement.

In 1991, Israel and all the warring Arab nations—including the Palestinians—began direct peace talks for the first time since the founding of Israel in 1948.

The Tet Offensive

Bold attacks by North Vietnamese on U.S. and South Vietnamese forces helped strengthen American opposition to the war.

U.S. Troops in Vietnam, 1961–1968

Year	Number of Troops
1961	4,000
1962	12,000
1963	15,000
1964	23,300
1965	200,000
1966	400,000
1967	485,300
1968	540,000

Source: Harry G. Summers, Jr., *Vietnam War Almanac*, Facts on File, 1987.

More and more U.S. troops were sent to fight in South Vietnam during the 1960s. More than 50,000 U.S. soldiers died there.

The United States in Vietnam

Shortly after Vietnam won independence from the French in 1954, the country was split in two. A Communist government led by Ho Chi Minh ruled in the North. Another government, supported by the United States, ruled in the South. The two parts of the country fell into civil war.

At first, the United States' aid to South Vietnam was limited to money and military advisers. But gradually more and more troops were sent. By 1968 over 500,000 American troops were stationed in South Vietnam. They tried to fight a traditional war, using their massive firepower to win. American pilots dropped thousands of bombs on North Vietnam every day. Army troops established strong bases throughout the South. But their enemies fought a guerrilla war, making U.S. firepower worthless. They ambushed U.S. soldiers and then hid in the jungle, escaping retaliation.

U.S. generals claimed that progress was being made. They pointed to areas that they said had been seized from the Vietcong, Communist guerrilla fighters in the South. They announced that large numbers of enemy troops were killed each week. While the North Vietnamese and the Vietcong were losing many troops, they ignored their losses and kept fighting. And once American troops left an area that had been "freed," the Vietcong simply moved back in.

Meanwhile, the war was growing more and more unpopular in the United States. Mass marches were held to protest the U.S. presence in Vietnam. Members of Congress spoke out against President Lyndon Johnson's war policy. In 1967, with a presidential election the following year, the country was deeply divided.

Helicopters carried U.S. soldiers to remote areas, where they could fight the North Vietnamese and Vietcong. As often as not, these opponents quickly disappeared into the jungle.

The Tet Offensive

In 1967, the North Vietnamese decided to try a new approach. General Vo Nguyen Giap, the hero of the war of independence against the French, developed the new plan. He would attack many targets at once and hit the cities, where little fighting had gone on. His goal was to shock the South Vietnamese government and perhaps cause its collapse.

Giap began by attacking a number of American bases, including a huge one at Khe Sanh. The American general in command sent reinforcements. But by moving these troops out of cities, he exposed the cities to attack.

Meanwhile, Giap gathered his forces. Each year the two sides had observed a cease-fire during the holiday called Tet, the Vietnamese New Year. Giap's plan was to strike during

U.S. soldiers carry someone killed in the fighting at the embassy. The Tet Offensive helped convince the American people that the Vietnam War couldn't be won.

A Leader Falls

The United States suffered 1,100 killed in the Tet fighting. South Vietnam lost 2,300 soldiers and about 12,500 civilians also died. The North lost far more soldiers. The exact number is not known, but some estimates suggest that from 40,000 to 50,000 were killed.

The offensive did not change the military or political situation in the South. The main damage caused by Tet was in the United States. People saw the strength of the North Vietnamese attack as a sign that the enemy would not quit. The commando attack on the embassy showed that no area was safe. It also shattered America's belief in the invincibility of its armed forces. Now even more people saw the war as unwinnable.

President Johnson began to reach the same conclusion. He decided to try for peace. Johnson announced limits on the bombing of North Vietnam. He called for peace talks. And he stunned the country by announcing that he would not seek reelection as President. Tet had toppled a leader.

this period, when his enemy didn't expect it.

On January 30, 1968, the day after the celebration began, the North Vietnamese attacked. It was not a single attack but a bold series of moves launched at the same time all across the country. The North Vietnamese hit five of the six major cities and over 150 other locations.

Most shocking of all were the strikes in Saigon, the capital of South Vietnam. Commandos hit many strategic sites around the city, including the presidential palace, military headquarters, and the U.S. embassy. To both sides, the embassy symbolized U.S. presence in the war. Nineteen commandos came to the embassy early in the morning, blasted a hole in the wall, and entered shooting. They killed several American

soldiers and held out for a few hours before they themselves were killed.

The U.S. army and the soldiers of South Vietnam were able to force the North Vietnamese out of the cities they had attacked. Most of the attacks were repulsed in days. The fiercest fighting took place in an ancient city named Hue and at Khe Sanh. The North Vietnamese were beaten there, too, although it took weeks. The Tet Offensive ended with the troops of both sides holding the areas they had held before it began.

In 1975, the U.S. embassy became a focal point again, as streams of Americans and South Vietnamese came there to escape the North Vietnamese, who were about to capture Saigon.

Operation Desert Storm

In a short war, a U.S.-led group of nations overwhelmed the army of Iraq, forcing it to end its seizure of Kuwait.

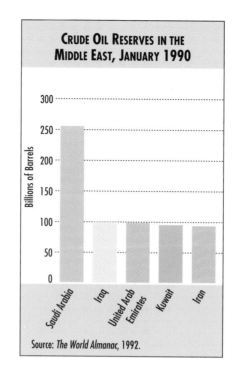

CRUDE OIL RESERVES IN THE MIDDLE EAST, JANUARY 1990

Billions of Barrels

300
250
200
150
100
50
0

Saudi Arabia
Iraq
United Arab Emirates
Kuwait
Iran

Source: *The World Almanac*, 1992.

If the seizure of Kuwait had worked, Iraq would have almost doubled the amount of oil it controlled.

The Invasion of Kuwait

During the 1980s, Iran and Iraq fought a long and bloody war over the control of territory and oil. Both sides lost many thousands of lives and suffered millions of dollars of damage. Iraq wanted to use oil income to finance the rebuilding it needed. But Iraqi leader Saddam Hussein felt that two Arab neighbors, Kuwait and Saudi Arabia, were keeping oil prices too low. And Iraq had a long-standing claim on Kuwait's territory. After weeks of threats, Saddam Hussein had his troops invade Kuwait on August 1, 1991.

The world became involved in this local dispute. The economies of the world rely on oil from the Middle East to function. The possibility that Saddam Hussein would control the oil of Kuwait troubled world leaders. Many feared that Iraq might invade Saudi Arabia next, controlling even more oil. U.S. President George Bush rallied world support to condemn Iraq. The United Nations (UN) banned all trade with Iraq, prohibiting it from selling any oil. Many battalions of troops were sent to Saudi Arabia to prevent a possible invasion.

Despite months of pressure, Saddam Hussein showed no signs of leaving Kuwait. The UN approved the use of force if Iraq did not pull out of Kuwait by January 15, 1992. The buildup of troops in Saudi Arabia continued. Soldiers came from many nations; the United States supplied the most, but there were also troops from Great Britain and France. Most remarkably, given that the foe was an Arab nation, there were soldiers from Egypt, Morocco, and Syria—as well as Saudi Arabia and Kuwait.

Desert Storm

The Air War When the deadline passed and Iraqi troops were still in Kuwait, it was time to fight. The plans created by the overall commander, U.S. general Norman Schwarzkopf, called for the fighting to begin in the air, to weaken the Iraqi defenses. Early in the morning of January 16, the air attacks began. They continued for over five weeks. The Allies used new laser-guided missiles and tons of old-fashioned bombs. The initial attacks were not in Kuwait but in Iraq. There the Allied planes destroyed control centers and communications sites so that the Iraqis could not mount an effective defense. It worked. Throughout the fighting, the Allied planes completely controlled the skies.

The only Iraqi move was to strike back with missile attacks. One of its

Iraqi dictator Saddam Hussein (*left*) ordered his troops to occupy Kuwait on August 1, 1991, declaring it a province of Iraq. After months of his refusing to leave, the UN authorized an attack to force him out.

prime targets was Israel. Saddam Hussein hoped that Israel would counterattack and that an Israeli attack on an Arab nation would drive the other Arab nations out of the coalition that opposed him. It didn't happen. Under strong pressure from the United States, Israel did not retaliate.

The Ground War Late in February, Saddam Hussein was given a last chance to withdraw from Kuwait. When his troops remained, the Allies launched a ground war.

The Iraqis expected a direct attack on the troops north from Saudi Arabia and east from the Persian Gulf. Instead, the Allies attacked from the west. In a brilliant move, Schwarzkopf secretly moved most of his army around the western flank of the Iraqis. He also dropped paratroops deep into Iraqi territory, where they could move east to cut off an Iraqi retreat.

The Iraqi army was overwhelmed. Soldiers surrendered in huge numbers; almost 100,000 finally gave up. Tens of thousands more deserted. Untold thousands were killed, either by aerial bombardments or by the tank, artillery, and infantry attacks. Within four days—100 hours—President Bush declared a cease-fire. The Iraqis had fled Kuwait, and the main strength of Iraq's army was broken.

▶ Gulf War success brought a surge of patriotism in the United States—plus thanks from Kuwait. But Saddam Hussein stayed in power and continued to threaten stability in the Middle East.

A Hope for Peace

Soon after the end of the war, Iraq was shaken by revolts against Saddam Hussein. But the Allies offered the rebels no help, and Saddam Hussein used what remained of his army to suppress the uprisings. Despite the Allies' hopes, he stayed in power.

Kuwait faced a huge rebuilding job. Iraqi troops had tried to sabotage Kuwait's oil industry, sinking oil tankers and lighting fires at hundreds of oil wells. It took until the fall of 1991 to put all the fires out. The pollution damaged the desert and the gulf. Black, oily rain fell as far away as the Soviet Union and damaged crops in Iran and Pakistan.

The Persian Gulf War, as it came to be called, was immensely popular in the United States. But economic troubles and the survival of Saddam Hussein lessened the sense of victory.

The most lasting result of the Gulf War may be its effect on Middle East peace. After the war, the United States was able to get Israel and the Arab nations to talk directly about ways to settle their conflict. After seven separate meetings, peace was still not achieved. But at least the two sides were talking.

Air power, surprise, speed, and heavy armor were the factors that contributed to the Allied victory in the Gulf War.

Glossary

alliance: An agreement among two or more countries to cooperate toward a common goal.

ambush: (*verb*) To make a surprise attack from a hidden place. (*noun*) A surprise attack from a hidden place.

artillery: Large mounted weapons, such as guns and rockets. Also, the branch of the army equipped with these weapons.

barrage: A heavy amount of cannon or artillery fire.

blitz: A massive air bombardment, especially the German bombing of Britain during World War II.

bunker: A structure meant to house artillery or soldiers and provide a strong point in a defensive line.

campaign: The movement and battles of a military force to achieve a certain objective or that take place in a given territory.

cannonade: A heavy fire of artillery.

cavalry: A group of soldiers fighting on horseback or from tanks or other armored vehicles.

cease-fire: An agreement between warring parties to stop the fighting temporarily.

civil war: Armed conflict among two or more political groups within a country for the purpose of establishing control of a government.

colonialism: The practice by one nation of maintaining control over people in another land.

command: (*verb*) To give orders to. (*noun*) An order; a body of troops under a commander.

communism: A political and economic movement created in the 19th century by Karl Marx; starting with the Russian Revolution of 1917, many nations adopted Communist systems in which the government controlled all economic decisions and granted few basic freedoms to citizens.

convoy: (*verb*) To escort or accompany for protection. (*noun*) A protective escort for ships or military vehicles.

diplomacy: The practice of conducting affairs between nations in a peaceful way.

emancipation: The act of setting people free from slavery or control.

expedition: A journey taken for a specific purpose, such as military service in another country.

fascism: A political movement marked by strong government control of social and economic life, few liberties, and intense propaganda on behalf of the glory of the nation; gained power in Germany, Italy, and Spain in the mid-20th century.

flank: Either of the two sides of a body of troops, which are usually the weakest areas and those most vulnerable to attack.

front: The broad area occupied by a nation's armies; in both World War I and World War II, fighting in Europe took place on the Western Front (where Germany fought England, France, and the U.S.) and the Eastern Front (where Germany fought Russia).

garrison: Troops stationed in a base or fort.

guerrilla warfare: A type of warfare marked by quick attacks, usually by small groups of lightly armed soldiers, against a small part of an otherwise stronger enemy.

incendiary bombs: Bombs that are used to start fires after exploding.

infantry: Soldiers who are trained and equipped to fight on foot.

invasion: The entrance of an army into another nation's territory.

landing craft: Vehicles that can travel on both sea and land, used to attack defensive positions on a shore.

left: The left wing, or flank, of an army; the defensive army's left faces the attacking army's right.

line: The position occupied by troops on a battlefield.

mobilize: To assemble an army and prepare it for war duty.

nationalist: Member of a group that supports national independence and strong national government.

neutral: Not allied with either side in a war.

paratroops: Soldiers that use parachutes to drop from planes to a position on a battlefield.

retreat: To withdraw or move back.

right: The right wing, or flank, of an army; the defensive army's right faces the attacking army's left.

rout: A complete defeat, or a retreat following such a defeat.

siege: A prolonged attack, usually marked by artillery bombardment and the cutting off of supplies, on an army positioned in a city or fort.

skirmish: A minor battle between troops of relatively small size.

soviets: Secret councils formed in many cities by early members of the Russian Communist Party before they seized power in the 1917 revolution; a regional or local governing committee in the former Soviet Union.

strafe: To shoot at with machine guns that are mounted on airplanes.

strategy: A plan; the planning and directing of the movements of troops and ships during a war to accomplish major objectives.

surrender: (*verb*) To give up or yield. (*noun*) The act of giving up.

tactics: The detailed plans devised to put a strategy into effect.

terrain: The physical characteristics of an area, such as a battlefield.

trenches: Long pits dug in the ground in which soldiers could stand and shoot; the Western Front in World War I was marked by elaborate trench systems that stretched for hundreds of miles.

truce: An official end to fighting, which can be the prelude to a formal peace.

ultimatum: A final warning that if an opponent does not comply with a specific demand, strong retaliation will follow.

Suggested Readings

Note: An asterisk (*) denotes a Young Adult title.

Asprey, Robert B. *The First Battle of the Marne.* Greenwood, 1979.

Bailey, Ronald H. *The Bloodiest Day: The Battle of Antietam.* Time-Life, 1984.

Campaign Atlas to the Arab-Israel Wars, the Chinese Civil War and the Korean War. West Point Military History Series. Avery, 1987.

Catton, Bruce. *Gettysburg: The Final Fury.* Doubleday & Co., 1974.

CNN Special Report: War in the Gulf. Turner, 1991.

Connell, Evan S. *Son of the Morning Star.* North Point Press, 1984.

Creasy, Edward S. *Fifteen Decisive Battles of the World: From Marathon to Waterloo.* Landpost Press, 1992.

Cressman, Robert J., and Ewing, Steve. *A Glorious Page in Our History: The Battle of Midway, 4–6 June 1942.* Pictorial History, 1990.

Doughty, Robert A. *The Breaking Point: Sedan and the Fall of France, 1940.* Shoe String, 1990.

Hastings, Max. *Overlord: D-Day & Battle of Normandy.* Simon & Schuster, 1985.

Hooton, E. R. *The Greatest Tumult: The Chinese Civil War, 1936–1949.* Macmillan, 1991.

Hough, Richard Alexander. *The Battle of Britain: The Greatest Air Battle of World War II.* Norton, 1989.

*Katz, William L., and Crawford, Marc. *The Lincoln Brigade: A Picture History.* Macmillan, 1989.

Large, David Clay. *Between Two Fires: Europe's Path in the 1930's.* Norton, 1990.

*Lawless, Richard, and Bleaney, C. H. *The First Day of the Six Day War.* Day That Made History Series. Trafalgar Square, 1990.

*Lawson, Don. *The United States in the Vietnam War.* Crowell, 1981.

Livesey, Anthony. *Great Battles of World War I.* Macmillan, 1989.

Macdonald, John. *Great Battlefields of the World.* Macmillan, 1985.

Monk, Lorraine. *Photographs That Changed the World.* Doubleday & Co., 1989.

Novikov-Priboi, Aleksei S. *Tsushima.* Hyperion, 1978.

Oberdorfer, Don. *Tet: Turning Point in the Vietnam War.* Da Capo, 1984.

Porch, Douglas. *The French Foreign Legion: A Complete History of the Legendary Fighting Force.* HarperCollins, 1991.

Roy, Jules. *The Battle of Dienbienphu.* Carroll & Graf, 1984.

Salisbury, Harrison. *The 900 Days: The Siege of Leningrad.* Harper & Row, 1969.

*Sauvain, Philip. *El Alamein.* Macmillan, 1992.

Index